DATE DUE			
Jul 7'82			

The School Library
and
Educational Change

LIBRARY SCIENCE TEXT SERIES

The School Library and Educational Change

MARTIN ROSSOFF

1971

LIBRARIES UNLIMITED, INC., LITTLETON, COLO.

LIBRARIES UNLIMITED, INC.
P.O. Box 263
Littleton, Colorado 80120

TABLE OF CONTENTS

Introduction

As one in a series of basic texts in library science, this volume furnishes a background for understanding the work of the school library. It is not a handbook of operational procedures. It is an exposition of the school library as a humane learning environment where the needs of students receive priority attention. It analyzes the nature of the librarian-student relationship. It considers the teacher and the librarian as ideal partners in a team teaching arrangement designed to give students greater scope in managing their own education.

The School Library and Educational Change is therefore addressed to both teachers and beginning librarians. For the librarian, it traces the development of the school library, outlines its objectives, and discusses the effect of educational and technological innovation on its emergence as an instructional media center. It offers suggestions for improving the library's reading and teaching programs.

For the teacher, this book illustrates how supplementary (library) materials are employed to make learning a more palatable and student-centered activity. It argues for a diversity of method that raises the interest level of students. The final chapter specifies the key components in a library collection which should be known to all school personnel. Thus, the book may serve as a guide in the in-service training of teachers and in more formal library education courses. The hope throughout is for a universal and knowledgeable acceptance of the school library as a powerful built-in agent for better education.

1

Definitions and Assumptions

For some time there has been a need for a manual that would define in simple terms the place of the school library in contemporary education. Such a work would bring up to date but not necessarily replace the basic texts in the field. It would summarize recent trends in school library development, paying particular attention to parallel trends in educational thinking. It would show how new ideas about education relate to school library objectives. It would reflect the turmoil and dissatisfaction prominent in current discussions about the effectiveness of the nation's schools today.

It is the purpose of this book to provide just such an orientation. It describes the nature of the school library—what it is, where it came from, where it is going, what it contains, how it is organized, and where it fits into the pattern of classroom instruction. It assumes that a central school library is an inextricable part of the school it serves, and operates in such a way as to further the objectives of that school, whatever those objectives may be.

A recurrent theme of this book is that the library stimulates the intellectual growth of children and is, in turn, influenced by changes in educational practice. Of course, the effect of a library on the behavior (i.e. learning) of children is difficult to measure. The changes in a student's behavior are subtle, internal, and of undetermined origin. Nevertheless, there must be some validity to the notion of a school library's power to educate. One of the criteria almost always used in evaluating the educational effectiveness of a school (in addition to the number of students it sends to college) is the strength of the school library program. Ninety percent of the nation's secondary schools contain some kind of centralized library. One of the most remarkable changes in elementary education during the sixties was the extraordinary increase in the number of schools providing self-administered library service for the first time. Apparently, the school library is considered a major force for achieving excellence in education.

A landmark study on the equality of educational opportunity—the so-called Coleman report[1]—concludes that the physical resources of a school have little effect on the intellectual progress of its students. According to the report, salaries, libraries, laboratories, and guidance services bear little relationship to student achievement. In other words, the study seems to indicate that the resources assembled by a school board are less effective than the resources provided by a child's fellow students. It is true that children learn from one another but a distinction should be made between schools where physical facilities are merely present and those in which they play an active role in pupil development. The report does not distinguish between schools where instructional materials are available for anyone with inclination to use them and schools where their use is promoted by the cooperative efforts of teacher and librarian.

The school library is an indispensable unit in any school, regardless of its educational philosophy. In traditional schools, it serves as an instrument for enrichment, student guidance, and escape from the formal atmosphere of the classroom. Schools with a more radical philosophy make greater demands on the library's services and resources. It becomes a workshop, a center for research, for independent study, inspiration, and communication. The level of its services is determined by a variety of factors: the size and devotion of the library staff, the instructional philosophy of the faculty, the structure of the students' schedule, and the attitude of the administration.

The library has always been a stimulus to students with superior academic aptitude. Today it is recognized as vital in the education of children with undeveloped talents. Recommendations for raising the achievement levels of these students include more pupil activity and problem-solving through the use of a variety of materials and more time devoted to individualized reading and reading instruction. Supervised study of individuals and small groups is stressed. The importance of the library in this context is obvious.

The term *library* is used throughout this book, although strong forces are pushing for a change in title. It seems no longer fashionable to speak of a school library. It is now an instructional materials center (IMC), a learning resources center, an educational media center, a "resourceteria" (!). The pressure for a change of name derives from a feeling that the library must participate more fully in the technological revolution, if it is to fulfill its mission. The development of a whole new arsenal of teaching aids (including the continuous loop, the cartridge-loading filmstrip, and the video playback tape) demands the kind of management that is the natural function of a centralized library.

This is the direction which forward looking schools are taking. New schools have accepted the philosophy and older schools are remodeling to conform to it. The question is: Can a school librarian be both a media specialist and an expert in reading guidance and library instruction at the same time? This question and related topics are explored in the sections which follow.

In spite of great expectations for the future of school library service, a number of obstacles stand in the way of progress. Everyone agrees in principle that, no matter how constituted, the library is at the center of the school's instructional program. Yet the fact remains that in practice most schools operate differently. A lock-step time schedule gives students no opportunity to use library facilities. A tight curriculum compels teachers to cover facts and ignore their meaning. There is a reluctance to depart from time-worn practices and a resistance to fresh approaches to teaching.

The educational establishment is notoriously conservative. Old ideas die hard and new ideas are regarded with suspicion and anxiety, if they are regarded at all. An investigator in the early 1960's visited numerous schools with the expectation of seeing many new ideas put into practice. He hoped to find an inquiry method which carried the student out of the classroom, a variety of learning materials instead of devotion to a single text, concern for the individual through differentiated assignments and grouping, vigorous discussion in the classroom with the teacher on the sideline, programmed instruction, and other innovations. Instead, classes were being taught with the textbook as the source of all wisdom and everybody covering the same ground at the same rate. Nor were schools with a high proportion of disadvantaged students operating any differently. Small group activity, individuals engaged in self-sustained inquiry, non-grading, and inquiry-discovery were conspicuously rare.[2]

THE SCHOOL LIBRARY AND EDUCATIONAL CHANGE

Educators are perhaps fearful of tampering with the child's delicate learning mechanism and, if so, their fears are justifiable. The precise nature of the learning process is still under investigation. Experiments are under way to determine the precise role of the RNA molecule in memory and the possibility of consciously altering brain wave patterns. Nevertheless, all over the country and in other parts of the world, new classroom techniques are being evolved. For it is inconceivable, with every other social institution (even banks and insurance companies) undergoing radical change, that the school should remain the same as it was twenty, thirty, or fifty years ago. The fact is that more experimentation is taking place in education than ever before. There is an excitement in education that is unprecedented in our history. Professors of education who cannot convey this excitement in their courses are obsolete. Indeed, it has been suggested that the study of education be placed in the liberal arts curriculum (where it properly belongs) and that practice in teaching be required of every college undergraduate.[3]

If there is any unanimity among the critics calling for a radical transformation of the school, it is this: Cease being a teacher and give the child a chance. Teaching does not produce learning. No child ever learned anything he didn't want to. Give him the opportunity to choose his own experiences and his own materials and let him alone. Be available in case of need and provide support when help is indicated. This has been the philosophy of good school librarians since school libraries began.

An educator, writing on the need for dialogue between teacher (or librarian) and children on children's terms, entitled his article "Attention Must Be Paid," a line from Arthur Miller's *Death of a Salesman*.[4] This desperate cry is the motto of every sensitive school librarian. The library is one place in the school to which children may go without an appointment and know that attention will be paid—where an adult will be present who will listen, and who will not judge or criticize. This concern for the individual child is the unique commitment of the school librarian. It takes precedence over every other activity, no matter how urgent the pressure of other work, the backlog of books to be cataloged or the bills to be paid. Librarians make themselves visible on the floor of the library where they can be approached and collared. They are aware of students at the catalog or shelves or microfilm readers who seem to need help. They are adult human beings, generalists and specialists both, who care.

2

The Librarian and the Teacher

A teacher, looking into the school library and seeing young-sters quietly at work in attractive surroundings, says: "In my next reincarnation I'm going to be a school librarian." Another teacher, addressing a group of librarians, wants to know: "What is there about your job that I couldn't learn in half an hour?" Librarians are accustomed to hearing these and similar expressions from their colleagues. They are bothered not so much by the tone of envy or disdain as by the lack of awareness implicit in the remarks.

Nothing prevents a teacher from re-tooling for school librarian-ship, if that is what he or she wants, except lack of time and money. School librarians are constantly being recruited from the teaching ranks. All that is required is an additional year of study and the ability to sustain it with sufficient funds. The hope is that such recruits will be young, energetic, and beautiful. As to the second teacher's remark, it typifies the common feeling that librarians do little more than write notices for overdue books and see that the books on the shelves are neatly arranged. Of course, they do or should do neither. It is partly to counter this mistaken impression that this book was written.

The point is that teachers are not familiar with the purposes of a library nor the methods used to achieve them. To take one small example, it is a common practice in school libraries to prepare lists of new acquisitions from time to time for distribution to the faculty. What should the librarian's response be to a teacher who approaches him with: "I don't know why you bother making these lists. I just throw them in the basket."? It seems superfluous to argue that a knowledge of new library materials, particularly as related to

11

his own subject field, is a professional responsibility of every teacher. How can students make use of the sources which will intensify their knowledge of a subject unless teachers know what the sources are and will direct students to them? And what of the teacher's own need to keep abreast of new knowledge in his own field?

This lack of a basic orientation to the function of a school library is regrettable, for it is the teacher who must recognize or create the conditions which lead to constructive use of the school library. Unless teachers perform in such a way as to compel students to seek out library resources, the library will be largely unused or become little more than a study hall. In this case, teachers must bear the blame for the waste of money and effort and the lost opportunity which a near-empty library represents.

The school library offers the teacher a method of so individualizing instruction as to give each student a job which he can do, using materials he can understand. It is the perfect instrument for combating the evils of mass education. It provides the student with a convenient learning environment, where he can proceed at his own pace, and receive sympathetic, professional help when he needs it.

A breakthrough in the preparation of classroom teachers *vis-à-vis* the school library is sorely needed. It is only too true that teachers come into the profession without any understanding of the school library as a medium of instruction. They do not know the materials in the school library related to their own subject fields. Nor do they know how to manipulate these materials for the benefit of the students and themselves. They are unfamiliar with the standard services of the library. They do not know how to motivate students toward books, to guide them in their reading, or to use the results of their reading to enhance classroom performance.

The institutions which prepare students for teaching must take the blame for this gap. Agitation for giving prospective teachers a knowledge of library methods and materials goes back to the year 1899 when a subcommittee of the National Education Association asked "whether the professional training of teachers had not yet reached that period in its development when the library must be one of the factors in the training of pupil teachers."[5] A few normal schools took the hint.

The librarian of the Central High School in Omaha (Nebraska) read a paper before the School Library Section of the American

THE LIBRARIAN AND THE TEACHER

Library Association in 1923 in which she remarked: "In my experience in high school library work, I have found the teacher a very important factor ... I should dread to work in the library of a high school where teachers doubted the value of books, failed to appreciate the work of a library and librarians—could there be such a school. The teacher who knows, loves, uses books, is the greatest support a library can have."[6]

In 1958 the Association for Supervision and Curriculum Development (ASCD) of the National Education Association recognized the necessity of employing a large variety and volume of materials in modern teaching. It passed a resolution in which the heads of teacher education institutions were urged "to consider seriously including offerings in the evaluation, selection and use of a wide variety of instructional materials as part of the program of studies for the preparation of teachers and administrators."

More recently (1960) the American Association of School Librarians accepted a resolution on "Teacher Education in the Use of Instructional Materials" which read in part: " ... the American Association of School Librarians, a division of the American Library Association, favors the introduction or development of instruction in the use of printed and audio-visual materials in all teacher-training programs ...."

The campaign has met with little success to date. Any attempt to introduce a course on the use of the school library as a resource in teaching is thwarted by the objection that the education curriculum has already proliferated beyond manageability. Prospective teachers are too busy studying the history, philosophy, psychology, sociology, principles, and methods of education to bother with the bibliographical content of their subject specialties.

Teacher education would be vastly improved if it included courses in reading techniques and library fundamentals. If the conversion of school libraries into media centers ever becomes a nationwide reality, teachers will need even more pre-service and in-service training in the use of instructional materials. Such training will include the experience of seeing good teaching via multi-media methods and of utilizing the various resources of a modern materials center.

However, it is unlikely that courses to acquaint teachers with library methods and materials will be introduced unless state departments of education mandate them as a requirement for certification.

Even if authorities on this level could be convinced of the need, there is some question about how such courses should be conducted. Can they be organized as separate entities and still be practical for teachers of all subjects? Is the informational content of such courses better taught as part of some other course—a course in methods of teaching, perhaps? Who is qualified to teach such courses—a professor of education or a practicing librarian? When in the prospective teacher's professional preparation should such courses be taken?

A group of professors in a midwestern university recently undertook an evaluation of the way American history was being taught in the high schools of their state.[7] They described the typical American history class as a dull question-and-answer period, based on information taken from an inadequate textbook. They criticized the course as poorly paced, with insufficient emphasis on the great issues of the present century. They blamed the situation on the poor preparation of teachers, their limited background in subject matter, their lack of familiarity with the basic books in the field, and inadequate school libraries.

To help remedy the situation, the professors prepared a well-annotated, inexpensive bibliography of American history materials.[8] They then urged librarians to acquire the books and teachers to become familiar with them. They argued for a return to that method of teaching which encouraged pupils to read books and to incorporate the results of their reading into the class discussion. Teachers were urged to take a more active role in reading and in recommending books both to students and for library purchase.

No great talent is needed to involve students in the use of library materials. The simplest method is to assign elementary re-search projects, the need for which is apparent and the results of which are brought into play during the daily class sessions. Certain abuses should be avoided. The stricture "Read a hundred pages in any history book" is futile. Nor should outside reading be limited to a few titles, some of which may be out of print or unavailable in the school library. As far as possible, the assignment should be cast in the form of problems.

In a speech-centered English class, for example, the teacher encouraged students to "kick around" a few ideas suitable for informal discussion. Before the period was over the class had proposed a series of questions to be investigated in the library and presented at future meetings as brief oral summaries and debates. Some of the suggestions were:

1. Are we experiencing a cultural or social revolution in this country?
2. What rights do students have in the management of school affairs?
3. What kind of education should students receive in high school?
4. How can we train for effective use of leisure time?
5. Should schools educate for marriage and family life?
6. Is college a necessity for everyone?
7. How is society dealing with the mentally ill?
8. Is the black power movement a danger to the social structure?
9. How can we help the underprivileged in our country?
10. Is rock and roll a serious development in modern music?
11. Is there a way out of the war in Vietnam?
12. Are the moon landings worth the financial expenditure?
13. Should federal aid be given to all schools—public and private?
14. Will the end of the war in Vietnam spell economic depression?
15. What priorities should be given to the funds which will become available when the war ends?
16. Is the population explosion a serious threat to survival?
17. Is there a real danger of a food shortage?
18. Are there any alternatives to the present selective service system?
19. Is the ABM an essential weapon for national defense?
20. Is the "hippie culture" an evil influence on youth?
21. How should the problem of drug addiction be handled?

A teacher of world history asked his class to prepare reports on the emerging "underdeveloped" nations of the world. The students drew up a list of the countries to be studied. They formulated questions to help pinpoint the information: What was the history of the country while under imperialist domination? How did the area achieve independence? Who were the leaders in this movement? What problems arose with the coming of independence? How is the area or country attempting to solve its problems today? Each student chose a different area for study. At the end of the time allowed for gathering the data, students pooled their findings and generalized on the conditions common to all the countries studied.

A teacher of American history directed his students to investigate the course of American foreign relations with specific reference to 1) Latin America, 2) Red China, 3) Southeast Asia, 4) Africa, 5) Germany, and 6) Russia. For the specific area chosen by him, the student was advised to examine these questions: What are the basic problems involved? What has been done so far to solve the problems? What criticisms have been made of past actions? What alternative courses have been suggested? What are your constructive suggestions?

A similar set of questions was supplied by a teacher of economics to his class for a research assignment. The key word "should" in each of the problems automatically required the student to draw his own conclusions from his reading. The problems assigned were: 1) What policy should the administration follow regarding the farm problem? 2) What policy should the administration follow regarding labor-management disputes? 3) Should the Federal Government expand or curtail its Social Welfare program (Old Age Insurance, Health insurance, Aid to education, etc.)? 4) What policy should the administration follow to best utilize our natural resources? 5) What policies should be followed to ensure economic stability and growth?

A teacher of English invited his students to select a well-known author and attempt to answer the question: How closely related is the author's work to his own life and the times in which he lived? Students were told to read two books by the author chosen and to confirm their impressions by reference to biographies of the author, histories, and works of literary criticism.

A teacher of general science scanned the index to the class text looking for subjects that merited more attention than was given in the book. After making a selection, she called on volunteers in the class to search out additional data in the library and to contribute their findings when the subjects came up for discussion in class. Among the topics were: abiogenesis versus biogenesis, alcoholism, atom-splitting, brainwashing, Darwin, diatoms, ESP, hypnotism, origin of the solar system, pacemaker, protein synthesis, protozoa, regeneration, Scopes.

Here is a partial list of topics distributed by a teacher to a class studying contemporary world problems:

THE LIBRARIAN AND THE TEACHER

1. Is China a menace to world peace?
2. What was the so-called "cultural revolution" in China?
3. Was the Korean conflict necessary?
4. Should the United States act as the world's policeman?
5. Who was responsible for the Bay of Pigs?
6. Why did the U.S. send troops to the Dominican Republic?
7. Can the differences between the U.S. and Cuba be resolved?
8. How was Castro able to come to power?
9. Has the UN outlived its usefulness?
10. Has the time come to admit Red China to the UN?
11. Is Nazism alive in Germany today?
12. Can East and West Germany be reunited?
13. Is the policy of apartheid in South Africa defensible?
14. Can Arab-Israeli differences be reconciled?
15. What was behind the Soviet invasion of Czechoslovakia in 1968?
16. What is your evaluation of Egypt's policy in world affairs?
17. What is the status of religion in Russia?
18. What is the Russian attitude toward art and literature?
19. Was Lenin a great man? Stalin? Gandhi? Mao Tse-tung? Franco? Tito? Khrushchev? Ho Chi Minh?

Whatever plan is adopted to bring or send students to the library, some form of follow-up is essential. The results of a student's investigation must be incorporated into ensuing class sessions. The method of presentation is left to the teacher's discretion. The least desirable method is an oral reading. Few classroom activities are more deadening than having students stand in front of the room and read their reports. An oral presentation from notes, followed by general discussion, is preferable. Even more effective is a panel discussion, with participants giving more than one side of an issue, and a question and answer period. A "Meet the Press" format is another excellent possibility. Above all, reports are never to be written, handed in, and promptly ignored. Pupils must see some purpose to the assignment and its relationship to their work in class.

Many teachers are loath to assign student reports and their reluctance is understandable. They find them dull and mechanically contrived. They consider students incapable of abstracting precisely the information desired and of presenting it in a stimulating and intelligent way. The reading and grading of reports is also a chore which they would rather not do. But students need more, not less, practice in this type of educational exercise, particularly if they are to develop a long-term ability to acquire and transmit information. The execution of a report, properly done, is a form of self-directed learning which produces educationally desirable results. While research-ing the causes of the Sino-Soviet conflict, for example, the student automatically learns a great deal about the history and politics of the countries involved.

The reports which students are asked to do should be more than mere exercises in the location of facts. They should call for some analysis and original thinking. One way of achieving this ob-jective is to suggest a comparison of several points of view, followed by an independent judgment. At the very least, pupils should be asked to give their personal reactions to the materials consulted.

The reports should be limited in scope and within the range of student abilities. Asking fourth grade students in elementary school to investigate the recreational pastimes of the Dutch in New Amster-dam before 1700 is out of line. An assignment requiring ninth grade students to search out material on the arts and ornaments of the Vandals in the fifth century A.D. is equally indefensible. Students should not be required to spend an excessive amount of their available time on a research problem or to seek out scholarly references found only in a research library. Nor should the librarian have to implement activities that have no educational value. If only one teacher asks his classes to read a minimum of two magazine articles on a given subject (and this is not an unreasonable assignment), someone must produce three hundred periodicals on demand, supervise their use, and return them to the stacks where they can be found when called for again.

The research report need not be a full length essay. In fact, frequent short reports are preferable and the full-length essay might best be reserved as a culminating activity in the senior year. Nor do the reports have to be in writing every time. Pupils should be called on repeatedly to deliver short reports, orally or in writing, individually or as a member of a group.

The preparation of a report—oral or written, long or short, individually presented or shared by a committee—is not easy for most students. A few are gifted along these lines, having trained themselves to be well organized in their study habits. But the majority need assistance and abundant opportunities to engage in this activity.

Teachers in general have not concerned themselves very much with this gap. They are too involved in covering subject matter and in acquiring conventional teaching skills to bother with peripheral activities. The process of learning to teach is of such a complex nature that it takes new teachers a long time to attain ease of performance in the classroom. By the time they have developed sufficient security, they are content with their established methods and are unreceptive to change. Most teachers learn to teach by imitation and by remembering how they themselves were taught. It takes an unusual teacher to want to deviate from established practice and to adopt an experimental attitude in the classroom.

Since many teachers, for the reasons given, have an aversion to the student reports or are not especially "library-minded" (as the cliché goes), students can easily be deprived of a beneficial experience. In truth, if practice in using a library were left to the rare teacher who recognizes the ideal library-learning situation when it develops, many students would graduate from school without ever having looked inside their school library. School librarians, therefore, frequently take the initiative in arranging research activity. They incorporate into the school curriculum sufficient library instruction to give every student some familiarity with library tools and procedures. They gear their lessons to the content of specific courses of study and seek the cooperation of the teacher in arranging suitable follow-up practice. They attempt to integrate library instruction into different courses of study to ensure a variety of experiences.

In small schools the librarian consults with the individual teacher concerned when students are observed floundering for information. An isolated request for help in the library is sometimes indicative of a more general need for formal guidance. In a large school, the librarian works through the department chairman to establish a point of contact between the library and the curriculum. But the most effective use of the library is made when individual teachers seize the opportunities for enrichment that arise naturally in the course of a term's work.

3

The Library and Learning

The nation is faced with many problems: war, crime, poverty, hunger, disease, pollution, racial hatred, population growth, mental illness, alienation, drug addiction, black rebellion, and others. Not the least is the problem of education. For unless we educate people to deal with these crises and others yet to come, there will be no people left to deal with anything. The purpose of American education was once defined as preparation for life in a democracy. It is now "education for survival."

What is the problem of education? Basically, it is a question of how to prepare students from different backgrounds and with different aptitudes to live in a world the future characteristics of which cannot be predicted. In this context, the old homework/recitation/test pattern which our teachers used and *their* teachers used before them has lost its value, if it ever had any. Yet teachers continue to require students to memorize large doses of information, extracted from inadequate textbooks, most of which is obsolete and most of which is forgotten once the test papers have been graded. This practice was inherited from an earlier stable period in history, when there were comparatively few facts to be learned. The question is now: Can this method succeed in an environment characterized by an unprecedented social and technological change, bursting accumulations of knowledge, and a disturbing uncertainty about the facts themselves?

There is no doubt that schools have been successful in the past. We have increased our literacy rate and shown a prodigious capacity for invention and technical achievement. Educators abroad look to America for leadership in education and regard many aspects of the American system as worthy of emulation. During the last decade twelve American scientists have been honored with Nobel prizes.

But weaknesses in the system are quite evident. Thirty percent of our students (the non-college bound) are not receiving the kind of education that will prepare them for a job market where verbal and technical skills are in demand. Students with creative talents are forced into an academic straightjacket of conformity from which they struggle to escape. Intellectually gifted students abhor the trivia which occupies so much of their time in school and out. Many are disenchanted because they have lost their individual identity in the mass education framework.

The chief criticism being levelled against the schools is that they place a high premium on the ability to memorize while by-passing the exercise of critical thinking. The complaint is not new. For years, educators have pleaded with curriculum makers to design programs that would subordinate rote memory to independent thought. Paul Woodring says:

> Teaching in its highest form is not just a matter of assigning tasks, listening to recitations, and grading papers, though all of these are part of a teacher's work. The essence of good teaching consists in providing an atmosphere in which children will learn efficiently, asking questions that will stimulate them to think deeply about things that really matter, and helping them to think more clearly and logically in order that they may come to sound conclusions.[9]

Putting it in terms of his own subject area, a scientist writes:

> There is the general problem in all science courses of ably teaching science so that it is an 'introduction to learning how to learn' rather than teaching it as a collection of today's answers to questions which will be answered differently tomorrow. The tradition of teaching and learning in most school subjects is that of memorizing important facts. To change this tradition involves developing a new attitude on the part of students and teachers so that learning becomes an experience in inquiry.[10]

What makes the situation even more devastating is that young people themselves now realize the futility of ancient practices. The emphasis on facts (growing at a rate faster than machines or the collective human brain can absorb) has added to their disillusionment. After a full day at school, they come home to a burden of homework which robs them of needed leisure pursuits and time for relaxation. They resent spending hours of precious time at home (and in school) memorizing useless information while problems of immediate concern receive little or no attention. They know that the world they are living in is a different one from the world their parents knew and protest that the schools operate as if no changes had occurred. A fixed curriculum (with no problems which students regard as critical), stringent testing, and an excessive work load have led to cheating, frustration, and a high rate of withdrawal.

The suggestion has been made that the schools transform themselves into centers of inquiry.[11] Instead of parroting someone's answers to someone else's questions, students will construct questions of their own, on subjects of meaningful importance to them, and proceed to search for answers from a variety of sources. The school library ranks high on the list of available sources. More than physical facilities for self-propelled investigation are essential, however. The concept demands a whole new attitude toward the process of education on the part of teachers and administrators. It means abandoning the notion that there is a right and wrong answer to every question and that the textbook (or the teacher) has the right answer.

The inquiry/discovery method (or whatever label is put on it) has merit but it is unquestionably impossible in schools that are without libraries, laboratories, or audio-visual apparatus—a condition prevalent in poverty areas. Here, too, are children whose intellectual development has been stunted by malnutrition and cultural deprivation and who consequently lack the inner pressures to learn. Nor is there any hope that poorly-trained, underpaid teachers will venture far from a mechanical approach to classroom management. A further drawback is the resistance to change on the part of those in control of the machinery and business of education. The humble classroom teacher is trapped not only by his own timidity and indifference, but by the weight of bureaucratic inertia.

We are all victims of a national failure to solve the problems of education that is appalling. Imagine the benefits that would derive from a national concentration on education comparable to the one which placed men on the moon or to the war effort in Southeast Asia.

THE SCHOOL LIBRARY AND EDUCATIONAL CHANGE

It is unbelievable that in this advanced age we are still uncertain as to just how learning takes place and what makes children want to learn and go on learning. An in-depth, money-drenched effort to find the answers to these questions would yield unlimited benefits but will probably never be made.

What is the alternative? We can structure our teaching in such a way as to help students formulate questions and provide them with the opportunity to find answers. We can stimulate their curiosity with counter-questions and permit them to satisfy it in the proper environment. We can make the essential resources readily available and assist in their manipulation. In other words, we can provide the kind of super-stocked library that has hitherto been a rarity and staff it with people who are willing to listen and become involved.

Imagine a school without textbooks, syllabi, courses of study, examinations, or report cards. There are only students, teachers, and a superb library. The library contains about fifty books per pupil (50,000 volumes for every thousand students); a subscription list of 250 periodicals; back issues of newspapers on microfilm; extensive resources in the form of tapes, recordings, films; and other learning materials. Students in this school are permitted to attend any class they choose and from which they think they can benefit. They may absent themselves from any class, if they so desire. Should we add (the *coup de grâce*) that the teacher's salary will be based on the number of students he can attract and keep interested?

Far fetched? Perhaps. But the picture is not unreasonable. In the matter of resources, there are colleges in this country with libraries that contain more than 300 books per student, with a far better student/librarian ratio than most schools, and with far less pressure on the library staff. On the secondary level, the library of Ridgewood High School (Norridge, Illinois) has 40,000 volumes for 1700 students or 25 books per pupil. Among private schools, the Fieldston School in New York City has 80 books per pupil (57,500 volumes for 700 students). In Windsor, Connecticut, the Loomis School has 58,000 volumes and 800 students (70 books per pupil). And in Kansas City, Missouri, the Pembroke Country Day School has 100 books per pupil (340 students, 35,000 volumes).[12]

As to the unstructured format which has been suggested, two thirds of the primary schools in England are employing a more open and free type of classroom.[13] The rooms are so arranged as to permit a variety of activities to take place at the same time, with few formal class periods devoted to specific subjects. Parallel rows of desks with the teacher planted in the front of the room have been abandoned in favor of informal groupings. There are no textbooks but books in profusion. Every classroom has a library and there may be a library for the entire school at the end of a hallway. Every child has a notebook and his own dictionary. A chart in the front of the room may list all of the activities available for the day and, for each child, every day is different.

The pupil determines for himself the activities he will engage in, the materials he will use, and whether he will work by himself or with others. Prescribed curricula and rigid lesson plans are set aside. The teacher is free to work with individuals or with small groups, to listen, to observe. In the belief that children learn a great deal from each other, the exponents of this method hope to make school a more natural and stimulating place where children at a very early age can acquire the ability to work independently. The assumptions (based on the work of the Swiss psychologist Jean Piaget) are that children have a natural curiosity and that learning will take place if there are materials available, along with the freedom to plan and choose. The presence of a teacher adept at organizing a multi-faceted school day, at ease with children, and able to guide them constructively is taken for granted.

An impartial survey undertaken on behalf of the Central Advisory Council for Education in England reports most favorably on the new, exploratory type of learning in the British infant and junior schools (for children ages 5 to 7 and 8 to 11 respectively).[14] The report has become an indispensable manual for teachers in these schools. When a series of articles by Joseph Featherstone on the British infant schools appeared in the *New Republic* (Aug. 19, Sept. 2, and Sept. 9, 1967), interested observers went abroad to see the system in action and returned with the determination to train teachers and establish schools along similar lines. Even the state of North Dakota, in a crash program to upgrade elementary school teaching, reorganized many of its elementary schools on the English pattern and is expanding the program systematically.[15]

Evidently, the curriculum reforms of the fifties and the technological innovations of the sixties were insufficient for a real breakthrough. What was needed was a completely new type of school where competition was eliminated, children were free to consult with each other, and learning resulted from a child's own desire to manipulate objects and satisfy his curiosity. If this kind of learning environment is successful with very young children, the question naturally arises: Can it work for older students in the secondary school, where the learning problems are far more complex and the methods of teaching more firmly rooted in tradition? Here, the greater disenchantment of students is met with more stringent regulations and tighter control. In some schools, boys may not wear beards or their hair long and girls may not wear slacks. Students may not participate in anti-war protests or go home for lunch. They need a pass to go to the toilet, to use the telephone, to visit the library. They react by adopting an attitude of indifference or withdrawing from the scene completely. If they respond positively, it is to publish their own underground newspapers or—in a more radical move—organize their own schools.

Not long ago a group of Milwaukee youngsters dropped out of public and private school to form their own independent academy. Ranging in age from fifteen to nineteen, they were among the brightest and most successful students in the city. Convinced that conventional schools were dull, removed from reality, and antagonistic to real learning and creativity, these students rented a ramshackle building to serve as a discussion center and library. Ninety teachers volunteered to act as resource agents. The students decided for themselves what they wanted to learn and how they were going to learn it. Emphasis was on the skills of communication and, as one phase of the process, each student engaged in some individual project of his own.[16]

One of the by-products of the recent revolts on college campuses was a rapprochement between teacher and student which never existed before. When classes were suspended, informal seminars and workshops were substituted. Discussions centered around the subjects of war, inflation, racism, and methods of achieving social and political change. There was a sense of involvement not found in regular classes. Habitual cutters attended the informal sessions with regularity.

Teachers, then, should ask themselves these questions: What would I do if I had no textbook, no syllabus, no marking system? What educational activities can my students engage in that will make them doers rather than listeners? What materials and procedures can they employ that will give them stimulation and satisfaction? Carefully thought-out answers to these questions will result in a meaningful program. The curriculum will consist of questions which students will raise and the procedures they will follow in a search for solutions. Since teachers can no longer know everything there is to know about anything (or even what is important to know), their function becomes one of helping students to identify problems and of suggesting possible sources where answers might be found.

The questions which students and teachers will raise may admit of no easy solution. There may be no answer or there may be many answers to a given problem. But the place to find out is in some sort of information center—a library, a laboratory, a museum, a factory, a greenhouse, or some other source. The library ranks high on this list of service agencies where research and investigation are conducted. It offers a humane learning environment, free of classroom rigidity and compulsion.

If these proposals seem too anarchic, in the light of today's educational climate, teachers may want to use some of the more moderate suggestions contained in the preceding chapter and elsewhere in this book. Eventually, they will invent their own devices for motivating students toward self-education via the school library. Their colleagues may be tempted to try comparable techniques and, in-evitably, the library will become what it should have been all along, namely, the center of the school's instructional program.

4

The New Education

More new ideas for the improvement of education were advanced in the previous decade than in all the years preceding. No phase of education was overlooked in the recognition of a need for change.

As always, the first area of attack was the content of the school curriculum. Groups of specialists, subsidized by government and foundation funds, rewrote the courses of study for every major subject. There were the Physical Sciences Study Committee and the Biological Sciences Curriculum Study, the School Mathematics Study Group and Project English. Specifically, their mission was to bring subject matter in line with the tremendous discoveries that had come to light in recent years. One of their major recommendations was the elimination of minutiae from the curriculum and the substitution of broad concepts. Once more, the acquisition of factual information was declared subordinate to the ability to reason. Facts were accumulating too rapidly for easy assimilation and transmittal.

A second important development was the application of new technological inventions to classroom instruction. Language laboratories (which have yet to prove their large-scale effectiveness) were among the earliest electronic innovations. Educational television, including airborne, closed-circuit, commercial, and ultra-high frequency channels, received enthusiastic support. Mechanical teaching machines— actually learning devices containing programmed information for individual use—were introduced. The 8mm loop was perfected. In the classroom, the overhead projector took over some of the chores performed by that more primitive visual aid—the blackboard.

THE SCHOOL LIBRARY AND EDUCATIONAL CHANGE

A third consideration in the readjustment of education was a theory of learning which held that there was more to the process of education than mere stimulus and response or trial and error. While our knowledge of how people actually learn is still dim, there was general agreement that no learning took place unless motivation existed. Students had to be convinced that learning was worthwhile.

This principle was nowhere more apparent than in the education of children from disadvantaged homes. The failure to reach these children spurred rethinking of our educational policies. Conventional methods were simply inapplicable for children who came to school with language difficulties, health problems, distrust, a sense of entrapment, and a feeling of futility. Children who lacked the social experiences that would prepare them for the traditional classroom could not submit passively to an alien, authoritative control. They presented society with its greatest challenge. Unless these children were salvaged, the cost (in more than just dollars and cents) would be far greater than the most extravagant educational program yet devised.

Massive sums were therefore spent on research, experiments, and pilot projects that would benefit economically and educationally deprived youngsters. Government and private agencies sponsored preschool experiences, remedial and tutorial sessions, supplementary educational centers, college preparation programs, summer schools, and job opportunities. Smaller classes and abundant auxiliary services were created to compensate them for their handicaps. Teachers were told to have faith in the ability of children to learn, for teacher expectations and attitudes could motivate students and have a salutary effect on their academic progress.

Finally, there was dissatisfaction with the old-fashioned structure of the school organization. The self-contained classroom was singled out for attack. Experimentalists proposed a series of modifications which would effect a more rational deployment of teachers and students. Teachers were to become members of teaching teams and classified according to their ability to handle large or small groups. Auxiliary personnel in the form of school aides and teaching assistants were to be employed. And students were to be placed in tracks best suited to their level of achievement.

A school design incorporating most of these ideas has been described by J. Lloyd Trump in his *Images of the Future* (1959) and *Focus on Change* (1961). Trump's basic objectives are to produce

THE NEW EDUCATION

individuals capable of critical thinking, intellectual inquiry, effective communication, and satisfactory personal adjustment. The vehicle for achieving these aims is a school program characterized by extreme flexibility. Flexibility is to be employed in every area of school operation: the scheduling of students and teachers, staff utilization, the use of facilities and equipment, and the architectural arrangement of the school itself.

If all of the features of the plan were to be adopted, students would spend twenty minutes at the beginning of each school day preparing their individual programs from a master schedule. The school day would be divided into fifteen or twenty minute modules of time. The modules would be linked into a chain of activities consisting of large group lectures, small discussion groups, and periods reserved for various kinds of independent work. Instruction would be carried on by teams of specialists, master teachers, and others. Some would be selected for their ability to address large groups, using the latest in audio-visual techniques. Others, skilled in raising issues and stimulating the expression of ideas, would be in charge of small discussion groups. At least twelve of the twenty hours a week spent by pupils in school work would be devoted to independent study. This activity would take place either in a conventional study hall, a library, a laboratory, or in one or more resource centers.

According to Trump and other observers, students can learn a great deal by themselves, as they are constantly doing outside of school. Students also have a great deal to learn from each other. School buildings should therefore contain specially designed rooms for independent study and for the exchange of ideas. In Trump's scheme, one room provides private study carrels with facilities for retrieving information electronically. Another has all the equipment needed for the preparation of reports: calculators, typewriters, duplicators, and even a UPI teletype machine or its equivalent. Conference rooms are available to give student committees space for consultation. The central library has the resources needed for work on advanced projects. Professional guidance can be had at every station. And for those students who need formal supervision, there is the old fashioned study hall.

The high school in Melbourne, Florida, is one of the schools which have put into operation some of the features of the Trump plan.[17] It is employing team-teaching techniques, flexible

31

scheduling, and the functional re-grouping of students. It has eliminated the conventional method of grade placement. It has adopted instead a non-graded type of organization in which students are programmed for one of five tracks (phases) for each of the subjects they are taking. The phases range from Remedial (for students with minimum achievement in the subject) to Phase 5 (for those of exceptional ability). Students move from phase to phase in accordance with their degree of mastery. Students of extraordinary talent are urged to apply for the Q or Quest Phase. If accepted, they work independently on individual projects. However, some independent study is assigned to everyone, regardless of ability. The amount depends on the student's capacity to work alone.

There are many excellent features in Melbourne's approach to education. Particularly significant for librarians is the emphasis on intellectual curiosity rather than the "fruitless task of trying to cover facts." The principal of the school speaks proudly of a "library that is larger than the gymnasium." In his opinion, students should spend half their time in a library equipped to provide aural and visual privacy. He advocates a heavy budget for books and intensive instruction in research techniques.

In this framework the library can become the vital center of the school's instructional program. This objective will be realized only to the extent that the librarian has the autonomy to plan with teachers for the optimum use of the library's facilities. His status must be that of a master teacher, materials expert, and curriculum specialist. He must be instantly available for consultation with students, sensitively aware of their needs, and sufficiently knowledgeable to satisfy their demands. He must have a staff of competent assistants on both professional and non-professional levels. He must have the authority to do more than the routine ordering and cataloging of books which others have recommended.

The John Dewey High School in Brooklyn, N.Y., is New York City's first experimental high school. Opened in September 1969, the school has adopted independent study, flexible scheduling, and close faculty-student contact as essential components in its structure. Students and teachers spend eight hours a day in school. The school day is divided into twenty-two modules of twenty minutes each. The entire school program changes every seven weeks.

Students are programmed for six, seven, or eight subjects in each seven week cycle. At the end of the cycle, the student is graded M (for mastery), MC (mastery with condition), MI (mastery in independent study), or R (retention). All important records are maintained and produced electronically. A master computer (located in a nearby college) provides print-outs for every need: attendance, performance records, individual student and teacher programs, a master schedule, and others.

Students at Dewey may use their independent study time for advanced course work, tutorial help, or the preparation of traditional homework assignments. During their IS modules, they may elect to visit the school library, any one of the resource centers attached to a department, the lunchroom, or the campus outdoors. The library serves at present in a conventional way but hopes in time and with additional staff to have control of all the auxiliary resource centers, the audio-visual aids and equipment, and the usual print materials.

Actually, only a small number of schools subscribe to the Trump plan or any modification of it. The plan suffers from a faddist quality and the fact that it was constructed by theorists outside the ranks of teaching personnel. Teachers need to experiment with their own ideas, utilizing the resources available within the school itself. However, the schools which have adopted some form of the Trump scheme are the pace setters. They recognize the folly of attempting to teach from a fixed curriculum in an era of extraordinarily rapid change. They see the wisdom of teaching students to think critically and of providing the materials to aid in the process. In this respect the majority of schools are years behind the times.

Nevertheless, the conditions for full-scale reform in school practices related to library service are extremely favorable. Library books and materials are being acquired with federal and state aid at a furious rate. Reading and the ability to read have a high priority in the school curriculum. Never has the intellectual climate been so disposed to improved and increased education.

Indeed, we are witnessing a thrust toward excellence in education that is unparalleled in our history. The struggle for quality education has become everyone's affair, not merely the exclusive province of the professional educator. It has claimed the attention of student, parent, teacher, and public official. This almost universal preoccupation with the problems of education is one of the most extraordinary and encouraging aspects of the current social scene.

THE SCHOOL LIBRARY AND EDUCATIONAL CHANGE

Concern over increasingly large education budgets accounts for only part of the public interest.

The 1960 volume of the *New York Times Index* devoted seventeen pages to the entries under the heading EDUCATION. Ten years later, the number of pages devoted to this topic had increased to forty-two. A new type of journalist—the education reporter—has emerged. The *Saturday Review* publishes a monthly education supplement which affords educators and laymen a superb overview of contemporary movements in education. Public agencies and private foundations are supporting countless projects for the improvement of the educational process.

The campaign is advancing on all fronts: curriculum, school organization, teaching methods, instructional facilities, and the materials of instruction. The school library's role in this campaign is one of total involvement. A major factor is the futility of teaching without reference to the constant explosion of new knowledge. While we have not yet witnessed the "passing of the recitation" or the "downfall of the textbook," it has become less and less possible for teachers to rely on these two media alone. Teachers of skill subjects like mathematics or foreign languages may be exempt; other teachers must constantly revise the content of their instruction. In doing so, they cannot ignore the assistance which a suitably stocked library can give.

The situation cannot be otherwise when we consider that whole fields of knowledge unknown a few years ago have become completely new areas for investigation. These include: ethology, biophysics, bionics, systems analysis, operations research, econometrics, ethnomusicology. A small college advertised a summer program for high school students in "quantitative and environmental biology," to include instruction in limnology, littoral oceanology, and crop ecology.

It has been repeated to the point of nausea that the world's body of knowledge is doubling every five years or even faster; that half of all we know in science was learned in the last ten years; that ninety percent of all the scientists who ever pushed back the frontier of knowledge are alive and working today. There are now 75,000 scientific and technical journals being published regularly. Four hundred new books and twenty-five thousand new technical reports are published every week. One hundred years ago the Harvard University Library had a collection of 120,000 volumes. This is the number of books it now acquires in a single year and this number

THE NEW EDUCATION

is not considered sufficient for the university's research needs or its reputation for high standards. The Library of Congress processes fifty pieces of published material every minute of its working day.

Within the lifetime of the coming generation, inconceivable progress will be made in every area of human endeavor. Vital organs will be transplanted with increasing success and artificial organs created. Molecular biology will decelerate the aging process and increase learning capacity. Hereditary traits will be altered or modified prior to conception. Energy generated within the body will be used to furnish power for hearing aids and artificial limbs. Space technology, a comparatively new science, has already made an enormous impact on meteorology, geology, medicine, and other fields. A television transmitter which can be swallowed in a capsule and used to send pictures of the stomach has been created. We have already built a life support system that will free man to go anywhere in the universe. We not only need to train scientists to perform similar miracles, we must prepare people to live in a world far more complex than the one we know. It is not enough to transmit information, even with the most sophisticated machines. Students must learn to adjust to incredibly rapid change.

An entire book has been written on the physical and psychological trauma which the individual and society will suffer unless adequate preparation is made for the onrushing avalanche of change.[18] The author places the major responsibility for training people to cope with continuous and accelerating change on the schools. Students must learn not only to adapt to change but to anticipate the direction of future events. It will be the job of the schools to assist students in making assumptions about jobs that will be created, human relationships that will prevail, and ethical problems that will arise. A number of research centers are already engaged in making these projections and modifying them as conditions change.

Five years after graduation from high school, the former student will have forgotten most of what he learned in school and the rest will be obsolete. No one knows the problems the future citizen will face. The best preparation we can give him is the experience of handling problems in such a way that he will apply similar procedures to new developments. It means providing him with the right materials under proper guidance in a suitable atmosphere. The quality of a school is frequently measured by the extent to which this service is supplied.

Moreover, students have no patience with drill, homework, and tests as the standard classroom formula. Penalties and rewards are no longer satisfactory stimuli to learning. Students are searching for new ideas and for answers to questions not found in the typical textbook. It is stultifying to limit their intellectual horizons to the platitudes found between the covers of a single book. We are living in a period when there is no one correct answer to any given problem. Controversy and a spirit of inquiry should be at the center of classroom discussion, with ideas introduced from a diversity of sources. Students must have the opportunity to think about and make contact with more than one point of view. It is in an atmosphere of free inquiry that student interest is aroused and democratic principles put into practice.

In spite of numerous pleas for reform, the schools of this country do little more than feed bits of information in minute amounts to children who are just not interested. The deadening monotony of this wearisome process is depressing to both teacher and pupil. It produces a body of citizens that is uninformed, unquestioning, and intellectually apathetic.

Few schools are preparing youngsters to live in a pluralistic world, to understand the problems of minority peoples and underdeveloped nations, and to work for peace and mutual respect. Many of the books that are found on required reading lists were produced in a world incomprehensible to today's youngsters. They are lacklustre volumes, written in an alien style, and with characters who perform few of life's vital functions. In too few classrooms are students given freedom to choose from a wide selection of titles. Nor are children stimulated to express ideas or opinions that are counter to conventional thinking. Students who question the wisdom of fighting a war ten thousand miles away or of ignoring a nation containing one-fifth of the world's population are suspected and maligned.

Most students are bored in school. Superior students particularly have little patience for the dull, mechanical tasks which comprise their daily learning. They see little value in work which bears no relation to their personal needs or to the problems of others. They flourish intellectually in an atmosphere which encourages wide reading and live discussion. A significant factor in the student dropout rate is a curriculum which is meaningless in terms of immediate personal problems and contemporary issues. Yet students are begging to be educated. The protest movement on college campuses and in high schools reflects a deep dissatisfaction with the content and method of contemporary education.

The school library's role as a center where inquiry and discovery take the place of rote learning is crucial. It is a place where youngsters can find materials to excite and satisfy their curiosity and give them a sense of accomplishment. If it falls short of expectation, the cause may well be a fear that students will question established policies too severely. A second and even more immediate reason may be a longstanding indifference to it on the part of school personnel. For teachers and administrators have never had a clear understanding of the real purpose of a school library. A poll of any school faculty concerning the real mission of the school library would yield answers as diverse as the individuals responding.

The complaint is sometimes made that school libraries are under-utilized and the accusation may be justifiable. But the responsibility for seeing that the library is used to capacity is a joint obligation of teachers, librarians, and administrators. Teachers initiate the activities which require students to employ library resources advantageously and librarians provide the assistance needed to implement these assignments. The function of the supervisor is to suggest suitable experiences when the opportunity arises and to encourage projects already in progress. He must also make it possible for the librarian to create a positive learning atmosphere and to function in the capacity for which he was trained. The library is too valuable and too costly an enterprise to be neglected or misused.

5

The New Technology

In one of the country's more affluent suburbs, $1.5 million have been appropriated for a new high school library. Not that the old library was in any way inadequate or sub-standard. On the contrary, it was an enviable complex, consisting of a large general reading room, several resource centers each concentrating on a different subject area, an audio-visual room, and a library classroom. It had a book collection of more than 40,000 volumes and an abundance of periodical files, filmstrips, motion picture films, and recordings. Copying equipment was available for the immediate reproduction of needed material. Convenient telephone lines made it possible to consult directly with specialists at a nearby university. A library staff of fourteen full-time members served a student body of 3,300.[19]

Despite the library's obvious superiority, the authorities did not feel that they had achieved the ultimate in school library service. With the aid of a federal grant, a team of twelve teachers was relieved from classroom duties to plan for expanded use of the school library. The new building plans call for centralizing all of the library's activities in a two or three story structure. In addition to the materials previously acquired, the library will contain two hundred electronically wired carrels. Students in these carrels will be able to tune into a bank of master tapes. The tapes are being developed on a variety of topics for students of varying abilities.

The leaders in this community are among those who feel they must plan now for the kind of school that will be operating in the last quarter of the twentieth century. While it is impossible to predict the kind of school that will evolve, they visualize an arrangement in which the library will be the center for all learning and learning materials. The book will be considered in relation to all other channels of communication. Students will be free to select from a multitude of learning devices. Sitting in his individual study carrel, a student will face an elaborate control panel and dial for the information he needs. The information will be relayed to the surface of a television tube or to a set of earphones or both. At the touch of a button, a master computer will furnish a print-out of the desired information.

This picture is very much in line with the currently popular tenets of McLuhanism. McLuhanites argue that the present generation has been exposed from birth to the emanations from television, film, and radio. Young people have grown up in an electronic environment and have been conditioned to a concurrent bombardment of aural and visual stimuli. It follows, then, that the school should exploit this enviable capacity for simultaneously absorbing sight and sound. Learning can no longer be restricted to verbal activity. It requires the total involvement of all the senses—visual, tactile, and kinetic.

The wedding of the verbal and the electronic was further manifested during the late sixties in the rash of mergers of publishing and industrial corporations. Manufacturers entered the education market in a rush to cash in on the new fifty billion dollar industry, a volume of business second only to defense. General Electric combined with Time and Silver-Burdett. CBS merged with Holt, Rinehart and Winston and RCA with Random House. IBM (International Business Machines) blended with SRA (Science Research Associates), the largest publisher of testing and guidance material. Xerox purchased American Education Publications, R.R. Bowker Company, University Microfilms, and the Wesleyan University Press. Raytheon took over D.C. Heath. Bell & Howell acquired Charles E. Merrill Books.

There is some doubt now about the wisdom of this impetuous and heavy investment in instructional hardware. At least one observer seems to feel that there are more pressing problems in education than the manufacture and sale of teaching equipment.[20]

Some years ago there was a vogue for audio-visual instruction, largely by means of films and filmstrips or slides. The flurry subsided when mechanical difficulties began to interfere with the smooth operation of the necessary equipment. Classrooms lacked electric outlets. They could not be darkened sufficiently to allow a well-defined image on the screen. The apparatus was not available when needed or it did not reach its destination on time. Even worse, the materials presented could not compete in quality with the commercial product in local movie houses.

There is now a revival of interest in audio-visuals as vehicles for instruction. The current technological revolution has introduced a variety of new educational media. School leaders are looking to the library as the most natural facility for making these materials available for both classroom use and individual viewing. It has been proposed that all school libraries organize themselves as instructional materials centers. These centers would house all of the school's aural and visual equipment. They would provide space for viewing and listening. They would maintain a central catalog of all the slides, recordings, films and tapes available in the school. And they would control the distribution of these materials in the same way as books and periodicals.

The idea of putting all of a school's learning materials in one place is not new. In 1915 one librarian wrote: "In the new high school library many of our schools have found it worthwhile to bring together all lantern slides, pictures, victrola records and post cards, and to organize them according to modern methods of classification and cataloging so that they may be available for all departments at all times." She also advocated the preparation of lists which would be sent to teachers showing what materials the library has in the way of "pictures, lantern slides, clippings and victrola records, as well as books to make the subject alive."[21]

The official position of the American Association of School Librarians was expressed in a resolution adopted at a 1956 convention. The resolution stated that the school library "should serve the school as a center for instructional materials. Instructional materials include books—the literature of children, young people, and adults—other printed material, film recordings, and newer media developed to aid learning."

The specifics for this type of learning center were spelled out in a report prepared for the Ford Foundation in 1963 by the Educational Facilities Laboratory and entitled: *The School Library: Facilities for Independent Study in the Secondary School.* This brochure contained some glorious projections of the future school library. It was concerned with those schools which had no fixed time-slots in the school day, no fixed pupil-teacher ratios, and no standard courses of study consisting of fragmented pieces of subject matter.

The report contained some noteworthy observations. It conceded that school libraries were still in a primitive stage of development, not through any fault of the librarian, but because of a narrow school philosophy, poor teaching methods, limited learning resources, inadequate physical equipment, and a low expectation of student achievement. It proposed a type of physical layout in which a student moved from the KEYS (card catalog, periodical indexes) to the COLLECTION (stack area) and then into a comfortable place in which to read or work, undisturbed by the activities of those still searching for materials. It opposed the decentralization of the library collection into subject divisions because of the increased cost of administration and because the search for information cuts across subject lines. A student working up a paper on paganism, for example, will hunt for books on religion, mythology, primitive man, and ancient history—all in different parts of the library.

One of the weaknesses of the report was its over-emphasis on hardware and design to the exclusion of such fundamental problems as overcrowding in urban schools, lack of motivation on the part of students, and widespread deficiencies in basic skills. It termed the teaching machine the brightest star in the constellation of teaching aids but admitted that good programs were lacking. It also acknowledged that any school which utilized a multi-media approach in teaching would require the services of a specialist in instructional technology.

It is certainly a logical step for school libraries, given sufficient space and personnel, to add non-print materials to their more conventional stock. There is no reason why a student reading about the middle ages should have to apply to the library for books on the subject, to the Art Department for illustrative slides, and to the Music Department for a recording of *The Play of Daniel*. It makes sense for all of these materials to be centrally located and administered.

One of the first public agencies to see the wisdom of placing all instructional materials under a single administration was the Newark (New Jersey) Board of Education. As early as 1937 it combined the library and audio-visual departments into one unit. By 1962 the Department of Libraries and Audiovisual Education supervised the operation of a Professional Library, textbook distribution, an audio-visual section, a school library services division, and a radio and television unit.

The 1950's witnessed the proliferation of instructional materials centers on the district level. In some cases, the district collections supplemented those in individual schools. In others, they provided the only source on which teachers could draw for materials to use in their own classrooms. Not until the 1960's did individual schools begin to establish their own instructional materials centers in appreciable numbers.

The instructional materials center operates on the idea that the information which a student needs is more important than the medium from which it is obtained. Print, film, and tape are equal partners in the learning process and, for the non-verbal student, the multi-sensory appeal of audio-visual instruction is particularly valuable. One writer argues that the opportunity for individual service to students is even greater in the IMC than in the traditional library because of the need for guidance in using the equipment. He anticipates the evolution in the future of an entirely different type of school library where the free distribution of noncataloged paperbacks will replace the library's recreational reading collection and where all of the information a student needs will be available on tape, thus eliminating the need for a standard reference collection.[22]

A number of colleges are experimenting with a learning center complex which houses in one building the library's traditional holdings, the data processing center, the television and radio studios, the language laboratory, the self-instruction cubicles, the "projectuals" preparation room, and the publications services. A few high schools are following the lead. The Wisconsin Heights High School (Wisconsin) with a current enrollment of 327 students has planned for a library of 20,000 volumes and facilities which include programmed learning materials, individual study carrels, a soundproof room for viewing and listening, tapes and films which may be borrowed, a conference room, a remedial reading laboratory, a language laboratory, four team rooms for teachers planning units of study, and semi-private offices for each teacher of academic subjects.[23]

Specifications for the South Hills High School in Covina, California, call for an instructional materials center containing an informal borrowing and browsing area, a reference and research area, an instructional materials laboratory with equipment for production and copying, an instructional materials library of non-book materials, and an electronics control center for closed circuit and broadcast TV, film and filmstrip viewing, and radio and tape listening.[24]

Many objections prevent the ordinary high school from converting its library into any such elaborate complex. The first is a commonly shared conviction that students learn more from the printed page than from any other source. Few audio-visual aids can match the mind-expanding power of books. Nor are the input facilities of any dial access system equal to the task of supplying answers to the myriad questions brought to the school library's reference desk. The range is from "Who is Nicolas Bourbaki?" (he turned out to be a *group* of mathematicians) to "Should priests be permitted to marry?" (more than a yes or no answer on a printout was expected).

A second drawback is the lack of personnel in libraries to handle the audio-visual program. Perhaps, in some small schools, it may be possible for the librarian to coordinate a library program for students with the audio-visual requirements of teachers. Most schools do not have librarians in sufficient numbers to do justice to the ordinary library demands made upon them. Furthermore, the audio-visual field is expanding so rapidly that it is becoming more and more difficult for the same person to maintain library competence and, at the same time, to keep up with innovations in the communications field.

The audio-visual expert or "instructional communications specialist," as he now prefers to be called, is himself on the threshold of a completely new breakthrough in the implementation of his knowledge and skills. Not only must he keep up with a rapidly increasing body of literature of his own but he is also expected to design and produce original materials in the form of mockups, transparencies and overlays.

The problem of securing and training personnel for jobs in school library media centers is currently being examined. It is the subject of a five-year study begun in 1968 under the auspices of the American Association of School Librarians and the National Education Association. The School Library Manpower Project is the second research program on school libraries funded by the Knapp Foundation of North Carolina, Inc. (The original Knapp Project, undertaken between 1963 and 1968, was designed to ascertain the educational effectiveness of school libraries which had met nationally approved standards.) Phase I of the Manpower Project has been completed and the results have been published as the *School Library Personnel Analysis Survey* (American Library Association, 1969). The survey identifies the various jobs performed by school library personnel working on different levels. Schools with well-developed media centers were selected to provide the raw data. Phase II of the project will utilize the results of the research in order to determine the kind of education required for jobs in media centers and how the necessary personnel can be recruited.

A promising development in library manpower procurement is the proliferation of two-year college level courses for the training of library technicians. Some one hundred and seventeen institutions are now conducting or planning library technology training programs. The training includes practice in the operation of equipment (projectors, tape recorders, closed circuit TV, and duplicating machines) and in the manufacture of transparencies, charts, and similar teaching aids. The hope is that much of the mechanical work in libraries now being done by professionals will be taken over by graduates of these technology programs.

A further deterrent to progress is the diversion of large sums of money to the purchase of talking typewriters and other cumputerized teaching machines. While experimentation and innovation are commendable, they should not be carried out at the expense of critically needed services. Practically speaking, it is more desirable to bring all school libraries up to the level of the best that now exist than to expend the available funds for a few privileged experiments. It hardly makes sense for the government to spend two million dollars on the development of a machine that will teach fifteen Indian children on a remote Wisconsin reservation to read, when the money could be used to provide books and teachers for a thousand times this number.[25]

Actually, judging from surveys reported in the press and elsewhere, no great changeover utilizing language labs and computers has yet taken place.[26] Instead of freeing teachers from routine, they have added the chore of planning and scheduling their use. Nor has any machine been invented which will train students to generate ideas and convey them to others. Educational technology still suffers from the basic truth that machines do not solve human problems. They are being used for the instant purchase (or sale) of stocks and bonds, tickets to the theatre, and passenger space on airlines. But teaching is a human problem, not an engineering one, and the teaching machine does little more than reinforce the trivia which so many find deplorable. Furthermore, the repetition of simple operations (or drill) for which the machine seems best suited will be no more attractive to students (once the novelty has worn off) than if it were carried out under direct human supervision. More probably, drill exercises will seem even more tedious when performed in an isolated, automated cubicle, away from warm, personal encouragement.

In an article headed "Time to Teach Those Teaching Machines," *New York Times* education editor Fred Hechinger comments on the findings of a Commission on Instructional Technology appointed in 1968.[27] The commission's report, submitted to the Congress in 1970, indicates that educational institutions make scant use of the media of communication so essential to modern society. Less than five percent of class time is spent in audio-visual instruction. Language labs are poorly maintained, broken, and abandoned. Industry has produced very little material designed specifically for education and what has been produced is of poor quality. The commission blamed the education leadership for its hostility to instructional technology, admitting that both teachers and students view it as one more step in the de-humanization process. It recommended the establishment of a National Institute for Education and a National Institute of Instructional Technology, with $565 million to be set aside for educational research. No action has yet been taken on any part of the commission's proposals.

A few schools are moving slowly into the new computerized world of education but it is likely that only a minority will ever reach the utopia envisioned, at least in the present century. The country is not yet ready or willing to make the investment required to create schools of such advanced design. It is only in recent years that the book itself has been recognized as vital to education and made available in prodigious quantities. The hardware and the software to go with it will undoubtedly have to wait their turn.

As long as money is diverted to the production of complex, educational machines, school libraries will struggle along with insufficient funds, personnel, and equipment, trying vainly to meet increasingly insistent demands. For, by and large, school libraries in this country are not providing the quality of service which present day education demands.

6

The Past Experience

The roots of the school library can be traced to the so-called "school district library" which made its appearance early in the nineteenth century. Around 1835 several states adopted measures permitting the purchase of books out of self-imposed, local taxation. The collections which resulted would hardly be called libraries by today's standards. Nor were they school libraries in the sense that they catered to the needs of school children exclusively. They were rather deposits of books placed for convenience in a central school building (sometimes in a private home) and intended for the use of everyone in the community.[28]

The primary purpose of these collections was to provide for the reading needs of a rural population. City residents already had access to the popular subscription and association libraries. At first, the school district library seemed destined for success. Books were acquired in respectable numbers. However, after reaching a peak in 1853, it began to decline rapidly.

The reasons for its demise are easy to determine and provide an insight into the pitfalls which hamper the growth of libraries everywhere. The first was a failure to support the collections with sufficient and regular funds. Original laws were amended to give school districts the option of using the money appropriated for books for any other purpose. Generally, the money was diverted to pay teachers' salaries.

Secondly, no provisions were made to fix responsibility for the supervision and maintenance of the collections. As a consequence, no records were kept and books began to disappear. Some deteriorated. Others remained in the hands of borrowers who were under no obligation to return them. Sometimes they were carried off by itinerant schoolmasters who claimed them as their own. Secondhand dealers did a profitable business in misappropriated volumes. Indeed, it was often impossible to locate the collection when inspections were made by visiting officials.

Because the profession of librarianship was still in the future, scientific management was lacking. The selection of titles was left to school board members who possessed neither the wisdom nor the diligence to choose carefully. Only books that were didactic or utilitarian were considered worthy of purchase. Fiction books, mythology, and fairy tales for the young were considered frivolous. Books on such controversial subjects as politics, religion, and history were avoided. A common expedient was the purchase of "sets," produced for the new market by enterprising but not always reputable publishers.

Finally, the school district library failed because it tried to be both a school library and a public library and lacked the resources to do either job satisfactorily. It did, however, establish the principle of taxation for the support of libraries and demonstrated a faith in books as instruments of self-education.

When the public library emerged toward the end of the century, it assumed the obligation of supplying schools with books for reading and reference. Indeed, work with schools became one of its principal functions. Various arrangements were made with boards of education, delineating the responsibilities of each participant. Usually the public library provided the books and services while the school board furnished the space and equipment and paid the librarian's salary. The books were selected for their recreational value rather than for any enrichment they might lend to the narrow curriculum of the day.

A small number of schools still look to the public library for loan collections or bookmobile service. However, as schools increase in size and the school library becomes a more integral part of the school program, dependence on the public library becomes less and less satisfactory. A library collection must respond immediately to the shifting demands of its clientele and must do so in strength and in depth. An agency operating from a headquarters outside the school building and servicing a number of different schools cannot be as sensitive to local demand as a unit operating within the administrative control of the school itself.

Classroom collections were another expedient initiated early in the twentieth century. In 1903 New York City appointed the former

THE PAST EXPERIENCE

Head of Work with Schools in the Buffalo Public Library to be its first Superintendent of School Libraries. His primary responsibility was the establishment of classroom libraries in the elementary schools. Sixteen years later his jurisdiction was extended to include the centralized collections in the city's senior high schools.

During this interval, the high schools had grown large enough to warrant self-contained library service. Graduates of library training schools accepted positions in these schools, evidently considering them to be professionally challenging. The first such appointment (to Erasmus Hall High School in Brooklyn) in 1900 marks the beginning of the modern school library movement.

Education during the first two decades of this century was a sterile and unimaginative process. The wonder is that there was any professional school library service at all during this period. It was the era of the Palmer handwriting method and the brief oral warm-up before every arithmetic lesson. When not otherwise occupied, the children sat with their hands clasped in front of them. Deep breathing exercises at intervals with the windows wide open constituted an advanced technique for the relief of tedium.

The early librarians spent their time largely in building their collections and setting up operating procedures for their management. For the most part they adopted the practices of the public library, modifying them to meet local school conditions. These processes are still prominent in school library administration and the question has often been raised as to the kind of school library service which would have evolved if the public library had not set the pattern.

Students in the first two decades of the twentieth century used the school library as a study center and borrowed books for their personal reading. On occasion books mentioned in passing by some stimulating teacher would be requested. In general, school libraries were small, uninviting, and poorly stocked.

Some signs of improvement in school library service were evident in the 1920's. As always, change in quality reflected the change in educational method. When chapters in some of the newer textbooks listed problems for further study or suggestions for collateral reading, book reports and student essays became popular exercises.

The formal debate was another activity which dispatched students to the library. There were requests for information on such perennials as vivisection, capital punishment, euthanasia, government ownership of railroads and other utilities, universal military training, and recognition of Soviet Russia. Radio, television, motion pictures, and the automobile had not yet cut into the time which young people spent in reading. It was possible to direct student reading by the power of suggestion. Librarians at this time also began to give some attention to the problem of formal library instruction.[29]

By the end of the 1920's, library methods and objectives had become sufficiently well-defined to warrant the publication of two books on the subject. Anthologies on school library management and yearbooks chronicling the experiences of individual school librarians had already been published. But the first two books to treat the subject comprehensively were published at this time. They were Hannah Logasa's *The High School Library: Its Place in Education* (Appleton, 1928) and Lucile Fargo's *The Library in the School* (American Library Association, 1930). With only a few exceptions, there is hardly a phase of contemporary school library work that was not covered in one or both of these volumes. The fourth edition of *The Library in the School* was published in 1947 and, although out of print, still remains a standard text in the field.

It is to the credit of these two capable librarians that they interpreted the function of the school library in terms of the great changes that were then taking place in education. During the thirties, many of the pedagogical ideas that had been brewing earlier were put into practice. These included a number of devices for adapting instruction to newly developed theories of learning and to the broad range of abilities suddenly discovered in the school population. Various names were given to these programs: the Dalton Plan, the Winnetka Plan, the Batavia Plan, the Platoon School—but they were all only variations of what was generally called the "laboratory method."

These plans had one feature in common. They assigned tasks for students to complete and allowed them to proceed at their own speed. The method had its origins in the so-called "Individual System" created at the San Francisco State Normal School for its own campus grade school in 1912. Here students were given the list of topics covered in each of the courses they were studying. There were no daily recitations or class assignments. Each pupil was promoted to the next grade of the subject after testing showed that he had mastered the work outlined. Clearly, some of the modern methods for individualizing instruction are not as innovative as their creators believe.

THE PAST EXPERIENCE

The reform movement in education of which the "Individual System" was a forerunner did not achieve universal acceptance or popularity. It was unsuccessful because teachers were not trained in the new techniques or because classes were too large or because it required careful planning or because materials were lacking. Nevertheless, it exerted a significant influence on educational practice. Desirable features were adopted by forward-looking school systems. Subject matter was organized into "units of work." Assignments were cast in the form of problems. An attempt was made to substitute critical thinking for rote memorizing. And a variety of materials was used to supplement the textbook. All of these features are prominent in education today. If they have not yet been realized completely, the reason may well be the failure to support them with good, centralized, school library service.

The school library was popularly referred to during the forties as "the heart of the school" or the "hub of the educational wheel." It is doubtful, however, that a single school implemented wholeheartedly the philosophy implicit in these slogans. The labels merely paid lip service to what may have been considered the library's potential.

In its 1943 Yearbook (Part II) entitled *The Library in General Education,* the National Society for the Study of Education spelled out the role of the library in relation to the social changes then taking place. It recognized the need for an enlightened citizenry if democratic institutions were to survive. It saw the quality of education measured by the quality of library service. It stressed the importance of reading. It pictured the school library as standing on the threshold of a period of extraordinary development in regard to the breadth and character of its services.

The school library never quite rose to these expectations. It plodded along, hampered by the anti-intellectual attitude prevalent during the war and the post-war period. Conservative groups opposed the increased taxes needed to build schools, pay teachers' salaries, and purchase the materials of instruction. They attacked the program of "life adjustment education" which had never been widely adopted by schools and used it as an excuse for trimming educational budgets. In addition, the cold war fostered a trend toward conformity which discouraged the open discussion of controversial issues in the classroom. The result was a neglect of school libraries and a disregard for the benefits of diversified reading.

THE SCHOOL LIBRARY AND EDUCATIONAL CHANGE

This was the period when attacks on the schools were a favorite national pastime. The schools were characterized as educational wastelands and breeding grounds of quackery. The attacks reached a peak when the Russians pierced the space barrier. Injured patriotism blamed the schools for permitting the nation to rank second in this contest. But no one pays serious attention to these criticisms now. For it is obvious that, if Johnny had not learned to read, write, and do arithmetic (as was charged), he would not now be succeeding in endeavors that shatter the imagination. If anything, the critics merely hastened the arrival of the extraordinary changes that were appearing on the horizon.

7

Standards and Students

For more than half a century there has been available to the schools of this country a remarkable agency for achieving excellence in education. It is a facility which encourages reading and motivates learning. It helps to diversify classroom procedures. It is the most natural medium for enriching the curriculum. It is a ready-made partner in any team teaching endeavor. It is a problem-solving area for all students and a center for personal guidance. But the power of this vehicle—the school library—to upgrade the work of a school has never been fully grasped or utilized.

The first set of standards for secondary school libraries was published in 1920, after a national survey of English teaching revealed serious deficiencies in the library program. The report, entitled *Standard Library Organization and Equipment for Secondary Schools of Different Sizes,* was the work of a committee appointed by the National Education Association and the North Central Association of Colleges and Secondary Schools. The committee was headed by a Mr. C. C. Certain, then Chairman of English at the Cass Technical High School in Detroit. The Certain standards stimulated the development of school library service, particularly after their adoption by regional accrediting agencies.

Among other recommendations, the standards called for the annual expenditure of $1.00 per pupil for library books and the employment of one full-time librarian for every thousand students. It pictured the library as a suite of rooms, "spacious, pleasant, centrally located, used exclusively for library purposes," with direct access to all of the school's learning materials, including those used for visual instruction.

THE SCHOOL LIBRARY AND EDUCATIONAL CHANGE

In 1925, again under the chairmanship of Mr. Certain, a Joint Committee on Elementary School Standards of the National Education Association and the American Library Association published the first set of *Elementary School Library Standards.* Here too the library was visualized as an integrated center containing all of the school's instructional materials and taking the lead in encouraging their use. In the opinion of one authority,[30] if Mr. Certain's advice had been followed, the management of a school's instructional materials collection would never have developed into a dual responsibility. School libraries would still be called libraries and library schools would have assumed the task of training librarians in the organization of both book and non-book materials. The need for audio-visual specialists would never have arisen.

As teaching procedures changed, and the need for library services increased, the standards were revised upwards. A major revision was made in 1945 and again in 1960. These two documents *(School Libraries for Today and Tomorrow: Functions and Standards* and *Standards for School Library Programs),* both published by the American Library Association, contained both quantitative and qualitative recommendations for effective school library service.

The earlier document defined the school library's responsibilities in four areas: the library as a reading center, an information center, a guidance agency, and a department of instruction. The 1960 formulation was unique in that it represented the collective opinion of twenty groups of experts, not all of them librarians. It established as a minimum requirement the ratio of one librarian for every three to four hundred pupils, a book stock of ten books per pupil, and an average per pupil budget of $5.00 a year for library books. There were additional recommendations for non-book materials and secretarial assistants.

The 1960 standards had no sooner been published than radical developments in educational technology and new ideas about school organization (team teaching, non-graded classes, independent study programs) made a realignment necessary. There was a feeling on the part of the leadership that the school library would be demoted to a subordinate position in the educational hierarchy (or fade into oblivion) if it did not keep pace with these developments. The result was the publication in 1969 of *Standards for School Media Programs,* a joint effort of the American Library Association and the National

STANDARDS AND STUDENTS

Educational Association, Division of Audio-Visual Instruction. Now, for the first time, librarians and audio-visual specialists were treated as equal partners in the educational enterprise. Print and non-print materials had equal status in the stockpile of educational materials.

The basic concept underlying the newest revision is a strong belief in a unified audio-visual/school library program. All of the services formerly provided by the librarian, the audio-visual specialist, the language lab technician, and other auxiliaries are now under one management. Instead of a per capita recommendation for school media expenditures, the 1969 standards call for an amount not less than six percent of the national education budget. In 1968-69 the national average per pupil operating cost was $680. Six percent of this figure is roughly $40. A media center in a school of 1,000 students would therefore receive $40,000 for current acquisitions, half for printed and half for non-print materials. This sum is over and above the amount to be spent for textbooks, reference sets, and certain electronic installations. Nor does it include money for salaries or basic capital outlay for new collections.

The new standards are largely quantitative. Book and magazine collections are far larger than any previously recommended. In schools of 250 or more students, the standards suggest a library of 20 books per student, but not less than 10,000 volumes. In addition, the figures for audio-visual equipment are a minimum of 1,500 filmstrips, 3,000 16 mm films, 3,000 records or tapes, 500 single-concept films, 1,000 art prints, 2,000 transparencies, plus globes, microfilms, programmed materials, art objects, remote access systems, and resource files. Separate standards for the teachers' professional collection are established, as well as recommendations for the number of TV sets, projectors, microprojectors, copying machines, and all the facilities for housing, showing, repairing, and distributing this apparatus. One full-time media specialist for every 250 students plus a sufficient number of supportive aides provides a staff large enough to administer the program. It was also suggested that the figures be up-dated every two years.

The educational goals of the media center are no different from those previously established for the school library. The media specialist works closely with teachers and students, selects and provides resources to meet the needs of innovative teaching, keeps teachers informed about new materials and educational trends, and instructs and guides students in the use of the various facilities. Students have an opportunity to develop viewing and listening skills in addition to the traditional work-study techniques.

All of the traditional guidelines for selection and acquisition have been incorporated in the 1969 standards. A written statement of selection policy is recommended for each school or school system. Liberal loan policies, longer hours, and commercial or centralized book processing are recommended. The necessity of supplying duplicates in sufficient quantity to meet student demands and curriculum requirements is frequently repeated. The standards do not insist on the central administration of the school's textbook collection by the media center, but they favor the idea if the needed staff, space, and clerical assistance are provided. As a concession to change, the standards now recommend that consideration be given to the multi-media approach in learning, the widespread use of paperbacks, the emergence of information retrieval systems, the latest research on learning, and the crisis of the central city.

Once again, the standards take for granted the kind of school where self-sustained inquiry is the accepted pedagogical method, where textbooks and rote memory work are downgraded, where students are involved in their own education, and where the role of the teacher is to put into perspective. By and large, the standards reflect a faith in the future growth of media centers that many will find visionary. They represent goals realistically attainable by only the most richly supported schools and dreamed about by the others. They visualize schools with closed-circuit television and their own TV producer and technician. The schools have multiple (supplementary) resource centers, each manned by a specialist and auxiliary personnel. The head of the media center is competent in both library science and audio-visual service. He possesses leadership qualities, administrative ability, and a talent for public relations. Each of his professional assistants is a specialist, some with a knowledge of curriculum and teaching methods, others with a thorough knowledge of print and non-print materials in individual subject fields. The members of his non-professional staff include aides who have training in electronics, bibliographic searching, photography, and secretarial skills.

The unfortunate truth is that few school systems have ever attained a desirable per pupil ratio of books and librarians. Many have not yet reached the minimums suggested by Mr. Certain in 1920. In 1960 the secondary schools of five major cities received an average of forty-eight cents a pupil for library books. Statistics released by the Office of Education showed that in 1962-63 school systems nationwide spent an average of $1.75 per pupil for library books and provided about five books per pupil in library collections. The number of librarians overall was approximately one for every 1,500 students. Despite a seeming improvement, it is clear that libraries have not yet been accepted, as vital components in the educational structure. The U.S. Commissioner of Education in 1964 called attention to the fact that three of our largest cities spent less than fifteen cents per pupil annually for library books. He termed the library picture in this country a national disgrace.

In 1968 the results of a four year study co-sponsored by the National Council of Teachers of English and supported by the Office of Education were made available.[31] The purpose of the project (entitled The National Study of High School English Programs) was to ascertain those characteristics of good English teaching which might be imitated by schools everywhere. One hundred fifty eight high schools with English programs known for their excellence were chosen for the study. The investigation produced a most unfavorable picture of the libraries in these superior schools.

Only two of the one hundred and four schools selected for intensive examination of the library met as many as three of the six quantitative standards recommended in the old (1960) standards. For a school with 1,797 students (the mean register for the schools studied), the figures showed an average of 6.9 books per pupil (as opposed to the 10 recommended), 1.7 librarians (instead of 5), 1 library clerk (instead of 3), a per capita expenditure of $2.28 per pupil (instead of $4.00 to $6.00), a seating capacity of 116 (instead of 180), and a magazine subscription list of 81.8 (rather than the desired 120). Yet these figures are far superior to those reported in nation-wide surveys.

In general, the study found that the book collections were mediocre in terms of accessibility and size. Less than half the pupils answering the questionnaires reported that the school library had all the books they needed. Two-thirds of the students preferred the public library, although the better the school library collection, the less reliance there was on the public library. There was a low correlation between the periodicals actually preferred and read by students and those found in the school library. *Catcher in the Rye,* the number one choice of students as a popular fiction book, was found in only half the libraries studied. Modern authors (Camus, Wolfe, Joyce, and others) were not represented to any appreciable extent. In one school library, six works about Faulkner were available but not a single book by him.

There are indications that a radical change of attitude toward books and libraries is under way. In 1963 a Presidential educational message to Congress contained, for the first time, a reference to libraries. A vice-president advocated distributing paperbound books free to underprivileged children as a sound investment for the future. A private foundation awarded $1,130,000 to the American Association of School Librarians for a project to determine the educational value of school libraries that have met national standards. But the profoundest impact of all came from an unprecedented federal commitment to education in the form of financial aid for instructional materials.

Federal support of school libraries began in 1958 with the allocation of funds for the purchase of books in mathematics, science, and the foreign languages. The move was an outcome of the desire to improve instruction in these areas so that the country might be able to compete more favorably with the Soviet Union in scientific achievement. The National Defense Education Act (NDEA) was broadened each successive year to the point where it subsidized the acquisition of books in the humanities (English and Social Studies) as well as in science. It also supported a number of institutes for the training of professional library personnel.

The greatest stimulus to school library development by far was the enactment in 1965 of the Elementary and Secondary Education Act (ESEA). This law was the culmination of a series of federal bills designed to help eradicate illiteracy, cultural deprivation, and vocational unpreparedness. Of the five major sections in this bill, the most significant for school libraries was Title II. This section empowered the Commissioner of Education to award sizeable sums to the various states for library books, textbooks, and other instructional media. An appropriation of $100 million was authorized for the first year of a five year program. Other provisions in the law provided additional funds for education projects in economically deprived areas.

The measure came none too soon, for the public libraries of the nation had become the victims of a voracious appetite for books and services on the part of students from every educational level. The public library had been trying for a long time to exert a more noticeable influence on the cultural life of the community. It had tried to do more than supply romantic novels to the bored housewife and how-to-fix-it books for the amateur home craftsman. A major share of its effort went into programs designed to attract a larger than teen-age audience.

Without any warning, the public library was suddenly transformed from a quiet, genteel haven to a noisy, bustling center of student activity. It swarmed with youngsters clamoring for assistance, information, and a place to work. Oddly enough, the library's public relations campaign had little to do with the change in clientele. The transformation was the result of new attitudes toward learning on the part of teachers. It was induced in part by their attempt to cope with the flood of new information. It was a turn of events which was unexpected and for which the public library was largely unprepared.

In 1961 the Enoch Pratt Library of Baltimore undertook a survey to determine the extent to which its resources were being used by students.[32] It found that one-half of its public consisted of students doing school-related work. It showed, as librarians had always suspected, that reading was the essential ingredient in the educational process but that no action was being taken to provide the necessary materials. It revealed that the resources of one of the country's largest public libraries were being taxed to the limit and could not possibly absorb the impending increase in student demand. It concluded that, unless drastic steps were taken, the education of young people would be seriously impaired.

Other public libraries were experiencing a similar drain. In some cases, students accounted for ninety percent of the public library's business. To cope with the problem, a variety of expedients were put into effect. Temporary quarters were constructed for the exclusive use of students. Teachers were hired on a part-time basis to serve as proctors and provide reader guidance. Special permits signed by the school librarian were required for admission to the public library's reference collection.

The majority of public librarians rose to the challenge magnificently. If they complained at all, it was to deplore the kind of assignments which students were asked to do. The assignments were often of little educational value or, at the other extreme, were completely beyond the intellectual capability of the student. Too often the assignment called for the use of the same book by all the pupils in a class.

THE SCHOOL LIBRARY AND EDUCATIONAL CHANGE

However commendable their efforts, the fact remains that public librarians were being asked to assume a responsibility which rightfully belonged to the school library. It was obvious that students were bypassing their own school libraries in their search for available material. Perhaps they felt that the school library did not possess the supplementary material they needed in sufficient quantity or depth. Perhaps they could not visit the school library at a time convenient for them. Perhaps they preferred the social service approach of the public librarian to the didactic methods of the school librarian. Or perhaps the atmosphere of the public library was less repressive and formal. Whatever the reason, the fact remained that the school library was not carrying its share of the burden in meeting the needs of students.

The infusion of large sums of money to strengthen school library collections will undoubtedly help to distribute the student load more equitably and alleviate pressures on the public library. Another basic requirement is a school library staff large enough and competent enough to handle student demands. The mechanics involved in the selection, acquisition, and organization of materials are time consuming yet subordinate to the real task of guiding students in their use. One librarian working alone in a school of a thousand or more pupils can exert very little influence on their reading or learning. In self-preservation he resists pressures for more and better service. It is incumbent upon administrators, therefore, to understand the nature of the library program; to provide the necessary personnel and budget; to free the librarian from chores which interfere with his professional duties; and to encourage classroom teachers to experiment with using the library as an educational tool.

8

The Library and Reading

Teacher A and Teacher B each have a "modified" English class. The classes are composed of students who on standardized tests or in past performance have revealed a less-than-average ability to do academic work. Teacher A has arranged to bring his class to the library once a week regularly. The librarian makes no preparation for the class visits because she never knows what the teacher has planned. The teacher himself doesn't know until the students arrive at the library door how they will spend the period. Aware of the aimlessness and futility of the visit, the class stumbles in noisily. At that point the teacher calls out to the librarian: "Show them the psychology books" or "Where are the books on houses and building? Those are good subjects for this group, don't you think?" The antagonism of the students rises; their resentment becomes more audible. They disperse to various corners of the room. Few of them make any effort to read. Some reach for a magazine and leaf the pages. Others just sit and mutter: "What a waste of time!" Meanwhile the teacher isolates himself at a table to correct papers or enter marks, ignoring the class completely.

Teacher B, on the other hand, makes the library visit a special occasion. Whenever he feels that the class can benefit from a change in the normal routine, he requests the use of the library for a period. A day or two in advance he canvasses the students for subjects that interest them. The suggestions are written on slips of paper, along with the name of the student making the request. The slips are forwarded to the librarian who sorts them out. Some requests are very general: a sports book, a romance, a mystery. Some are very specific: the new sound in music, a book about billiards, the story of a convict or criminal. A few ask for specific titles.

When the students arrive for their visit, they find the books grouped on the library tables. After they are seated, the librarian talks to them about the books that have been selected. He distributes the books that have been requested. After all the special orders have been filled, the librarian stops to permit the other students to make their selection. He and the teacher move around the room, assisting the more hesitant readers. A few are directed or escorted to designated shelves in the library. Before the period ends, everyone has made a choice and borrowed the book for reading in class or at home.

This plan is standard in school libraries. It requires a little advance planning and cooperation between teacher and librarian. The difference in attitude on the part of students is apparent when the teacher takes the time to plan with the students a productive book selection period and assists in its implementation.

The scheme can be adopted by teachers of any subject. A science teacher requires his students to read one book on any phase of biology. He schedules his classes to the library, after checking with the librarian. When the classes arrive, they find an attractive assortment of new books ready for them. Small, hand-lettered signs on each table designate the topics represented: One reads: **Evolution— Genetics—Heredity**. Another is marked: **Anthropology—Palaeontology**. A third has: **Biology—Ecology—Psychology**. A fourth: **Microscopy— Physiology—Biochemistry—The Cell**. On the fifth: **Medicine and Health**. The sixth: **Biographies**. This device simplifies selection, saves random ambling, yet allows some latitude for browsing. The librarian addresses the groups at the beginning of the period, pointing out the subject breakdown, and calling attention to particularly enticing items.

Librarians can suggest to teachers a variety of themes around which supplementary reading can be based. The school library may be strong in certain areas and the books in these sections can be promoted in this way. Typical reading cores are: Folklore and Legend, American Humor, Popularized Science, True Adventure, Real Episodes in History. Fiction is not neglected: Mystery, Historical Novels, Contemporary Authors.

If a visit to the library is not feasible, books may be sent to the classroom. The best procedure here is for the librarian to accompany the books and to talk about them to the class. In an emergency, if the librarian cannot be spared, a student aide can wheel the books into the room and the teacher can take over. Circulation of the books to individual students is simplified if they are stamped (with the date due) before they leave the library. Students make their selections and sign for them in class. Before the period ends, the cards for the books borrowed are sent to the library along with the books not chosen.

In presenting books to students, the time-tested practice of "book talks" is an effective way of motivating students to read. This device requires considerably more preparation by the librarian than the casual presentations just described. It is especially successful when librarians have given such book talks frequently enough to have acquired the necessary skills. In these presentations, the librarian may employ one of several techniques. He may select five or six books of dramatic quality and relate an incident from each using a common theme and skillful transitions. He then mentions other titles of equal interest that have been assembled. Or a large number of books may be orally annotated and distributed to individuals as interest in them is revealed.

Two practical handbooks to assist teachers and librarians in the preparation of successful book talks are: *Juniorplots, a Book Talk Manual for Teachers and Librarians* (Bowker, 1967) and *Introducing Books, a Guide for the Middle Grades* (Bowker, 1970), both by John Gillespie and Diana Lembo. The books included have been grouped thematically (making friends, emotional growth, physical problems, earning a living, developing a world view, achieving self-reliance, etc.) and most of them are recent and popular with young people. The plot analyses are fairly detailed and the related titles recommended for additional reading are well chosen. Suggestions for conducting effective book talks are contained in the introductions. The second volume lists a few films, filmstrips, and recordings to be used along with the books mentioned.

A successful series of book talks was developed by one librarian in this way. The first session revolved around the topic: "Where did man come from?" Books dealing with fossils, primitive man, and evolution were selected. The librarian's talk was centered around the various theories of man's origins and the life of Darwin. Recent discoveries of human fossils were mentioned. Each of the relevant books were opened to colorful illustrations in the course of the presentation.

THE SCHOOL LIBRARY AND EDUCATIONAL CHANGE

In a follow-up session, the talk related to the topic of: "What are some of the unusual activities in which men are engaged today?" Here, books dealing with unusual occupations and the biographies of exceptional personalities were introduced. A later talk was developed around the theme: "Where is man heading?" This session considered books on space travel, deep sea exploration, and science fiction.

These are a few of the group techniques employed by teachers and librarians to encourage reading in English and other subject classes. We shall see in a later chapter how the librarian works with individual students to help satisfy a specific reading hunger. It is reasonable to assume that any program for the improvement of reading is severely handicapped without the services of a well-stocked library and willing staff. The good school library offers students the opportunity to hear about books, to browse freely and select books at will, to receive advice, and to read in an atmosphere created for that purpose.

Even at the earliest level, children can benefit from the reading services of the school library. Children in the primary grades are brought to the library for story hours, picture book hours, and book selection. Regardless of the method used to teach them to read, it is only through exposure to a variety of books that they acquire the taste and pleasure of reading. Many of them soon grasp the fundamentals and outgrow the basal reader. They need fresh material to keep interest alive. A collection of books in a corner of the classroom, drawn from the central library and changed frequently, gives them a chance to read extensively while the teacher works with other groups.

For many years a controversy has raged over the best way to teach children to read—whether the stress should be on phonics (the relationship between letters and their sounds) or on the recognition of words and their meaning.[33] The chances are that different pupils learn to read in different ways and at different speeds and that the teacher is more important than the method. Current trends favor an emphasis on phonics, without ignoring meaning, at least in the beginning stages and with pupils from disadvantaged areas. A reading series—readiness text, workbook, pre-primer, primer, and reader—provides the instructional basis for sequential growth in reading power.

There has been considerable criticism of the basal reading series. The readers have been characterized as dull and irrelevant to the lives of economically depressed, city-bred children. Teachers tend to depend on them too heavily and to belabor points that do not need excessive drill. The readers make for a regimented form of instruction which does not allow for the imbalance in learning rate present in any group. A number of reforms have been suggested.

One commendable innovation has been the adoption of a plan long favored by librarians. This is the Individualized Reading Program which permits the child to choose his own reading material from a vast assortment. In its purest form, the Individualized Reading Program replaces completely the phonics or word-meaning methods. With each child reading a different book, the teacher acts as a consultant or coach, giving as much individual help as time and the size of the class permit. More often, individualized reading is used as a supplement to the basal reader.

However used, whether as a supplement or in lieu of some other method, individualized reading calls for the support of a strong central collection. About fifteen years ago an adaptation of the individualized reading method was introduced at James Madison High School in Brooklyn, New York. Students who were under-average but not severely retarded in reading ability were placed in classes where silent reading was the dominant activity. The reading class was substituted for the regular English class which the student would normally be attending.

A variety of devices were used to make reading a more normal and pleasurable experience for these youngsters. The chief attraction was a copious supply of paperbound books available in the school library. Students were given permission to visit the library during class periods as frequently as was necessary. They were required only to select a book which they thought they would enjoy and to bring the book with them to class every day.

The success of such a program depends quite naturally on the involvement of the teacher in the student's reading and writing. He cannot use class time for his own purpose—to correct papers or prepare lessons. The period has to be devoted to consultation with as many students as possible. The individual conferences are brief interviews during which encouragement is given and the entries in the student's journal are corrected. The journal is an integral part of the program, consisting of the student's reactions to the book he is reading.

THE SCHOOL LIBRARY AND EDUCATIONAL CHANGE

When the program first began, the library treated the paper-bound book collection in more or less standard fashion. A record was kept of the number of copies of each title purchased. A date pocket was pasted into each book and a book card prepared. The books were loaned on signature in the same way as all other books and the same regulations for the return of books applied. The only difference was in the shelving of the books. They were kept in racks purchased for the purpose and apart from the regular collection.

As the program developed and large quantities of paperbounds were acquired, it was decided that formal records were too time-consuming. Lending procedures were also drastically relaxed. The only processing which the books received consisted of rubber-stamping the name of the library inside the front cover and the date due in the back. This is the plan currently in progress. Signatures are no longer required from borrowers. No circulation records are kept and no overdue notices are sent. The student is on his honor to return the book when he has finished. If he fails to do so, the loss is not disastrous. The books are considered expendable.

A popular periodical in the media field awarded a five dollar prize not long ago to a teacher who submitted this original idea. He suggested that honors classes be permitted the luxury of a free silent reading period once a week, during which students would be allowed to read any book that was not required for any course in the school. The question naturally arises: why only once a week? Or why just for honors classes? The idea is not exactly new. The trouble is that administrators have to be convinced that the student is not wasting time. Even more, what is the teacher doing during this period to earn his salary?

A few years ago a group of professors at the University of Michigan were commissioned to construct an English curriculum for one of the state's correctional schools for boys. They adopted the slogan "English in Every Classroom" and held the teacher of every subject responsible for language instruction in his own area. Newspapers, original writing, magazines, and paperback books were at the core of the English program itself. The school library book collection consisted entirely of paperbacks—7,500 books for 280 boys.

The Fader plan—as it has come to be known, after its principal architect—has been described in the preliminary report *Hooked on Books* by D.N. Fader and Morton Shaevitz (Berkley, 1966) and in the

THE LIBRARY AND READING

revised *Hooked on Books: Program and Proof* by D.N. Fader and E.B. McNeill (Berkley, 1968). A list of five hundred paperbacks favored by teenagers was published in the original volume and enlarged to a reading list of a thousand titles in the later edition. What is especially noteworthy in the lists is the presence of large numbers of books by and about Negroes. The boys in this school read with intensity such volumes as Braithwaite's *To Sir, with Love,* Dick Gregory's *Nigger* and *From the Back of the Bus,* Griffin's *Black like Me,* Ralph Ellison's *Invisible Man,* Warren Miller's *The Cool World,* Richard Wright's *Black Boy* and *Native Son,* and the pungent novels of Chester Himes.

A librarian in a Detroit high school with a large percentage of students from slum areas reports marked success with the Fader plan.[34] Taking her cue from Fader's premise that children associate failure with the hardbound textbook anthology, this librarian launched a reading program which fed paperbound books and magazines to students freely. She attributes her success to the availability of such titles as those mentioned above. She recognized the need which her students had to relate to the characters and action in these books and acted accordingly, establishing an enviable point of contact between herself and her readers.

The librarian in a school is often in a more favorable position to deal with the disadvantaged student than his colleague in the classroom. He knows that somewhere in the vast storehouse under his control there must be something which will strike a response in any student, however frustrated. A picture history of the civil rights movement will appeal to one. Another will settle for nothing less than a volume on black nationalism—no middle road for him. A third wants to be left strictly alone, to make his own discovery and choice.

Sometimes, a book and a reader will connect in a totally unexpected way. A teacher who sent a pupil messenger to the library for a copy of Herndon's *The Way It Spozed to Be* had to forego the pleasure of reading it temporarily. On his way back to class with the book, the student was attracted to the cover. When he reached the classroom, he took his seat and began reading the book. Completely spellbound, he begged to be allowed to finish the book at home.

Librarians who are uneasy about acquiring some of the books which deprived youngsters are demanding because of their unconventional language or sordid settings need to reconsider their position. We are witnessing a tendency toward frankness and naturalism in all of the mass media—in publishing, television, motion pictures, and the theatre.

THE SCHOOL LIBRARY AND EDUCATIONAL CHANGE

No one is suggesting that librarians invest in pornography. We are suggesting that books which caused a few eyebrows to lift a short while ago are now acceptable and being read by readers without injury to themselves or their psyches. Young people too are far more casual in their reactions to the facts of life than their elders. Of course, librarians in communities which have censored such fine books as *To Kill a Mockingbird, The Good Earth* and *The Catcher in the Rye* have a special problem.

Although we are on the road to providing youth with an uncensored supply of every kind of reading matter, we have not as yet reached that goal. There are those who feel that, if literature can have beneficial effects, it can also be injurious. Librarians are therefore unhappy about acquiring books that treat sex, drugs, and politics with frankness. In this connection, it should be noted that a preliminary report by a presidential commission studying the effects of pornography and obscenity has concluded that youth is not being corrupted by erotic films and books.[35] The final draft was delayed in publication, possibly because the commission's members were not in agreement or because the administration has repudiated it. Nevertheless, as reported in the press, the commission has found that "there is no evidence that exposure to pornography operates as a cause of misconduct in either youths or adults." Despite a wave of explicit sex in books, magazines and films over the past decade, there has been no increase in sex crimes. At its midwinter conference in January 1971, the American Library Association commended the commission for its report and urged the President and Senate of the United States to reconsider their categorical rejection of the findings.

At an institute on Intellectual Freedom and the Teenager held in 1967, three groups within the American Library Association had already reached the conclusion that there was no evidence of a correlation between juvenile delinquency and obscene materials.[36] The basis for the conclusion rested on arguments by authorities that juvenile delinquents were not readers and that young people tended to ignore material they did not understand. As a result of the deliberations, one of the provisions in the Library Bill of Rights (an American Library Association statement originally adopted in 1948) was amended to include the word "age". Paragraph 5 of this document now reads: "The rights of an individual to the use of a library should not be denied or abridged because of his age, race, religion, national origins or social or political views."

9

Library Instruction

The problem of teaching basic library skills to students has received scant attention in professional literature. The subject has been avoided perhaps on the ground that there is nothing complex or mysterious about it. It may be that librarians have been too occupied with the ordinary operations of the library to give much thought to their teaching obligations. In any event, there has been little formal research on the content of library instruction, the methods used, the relative effectiveness of the different approaches, or the benefits to be derived.

A recurrent theme in contemporary thinking about library instruction is that it is no longer defensible to teach students the mechanics of library research. According to the chief apologist for this point of view, the sum total of human knowledge is expanding at such an exponential rate that only specialists can cope with the retrieval process. Students should not waste their time looking for information when the body of knowledge has become so massive and the keys to its location have become so complex. They should instead apply to professionals who will supply the information desired in its original form or in facsimile. The student's time is better spent in analyzing the information obtained rather than in wasted motion trying to locate it. Possessing amateur research skills at best, he might easily fail to discover the optimum source for his needs.

An opposing opinion holds that, with the new emphasis on individualized learning through independent study and reading, students need to strengthen their ability to do library research more than ever. Nor should students be deprived of the pleasure of discovery.

THE SCHOOL LIBRARY AND EDUCATIONAL CHANGE

In fact, the process of inquiry may have more educational value than any single piece of information which the student may need. Nor have the tools of research in a school library become so complex as to be beyond the powers of the average student. If they have, they had better be simplified. It is also important to distinguish between the urgent need of a toxicologist searching electronically for the antidote to a specific poison and a student's request for a copy of Kipling's *Gunga Din.*

The present consensus is that there is value in formal library instruction and that, when given, it should be completely integrated with a specific research problem or curriculum unit. Even on the elementary level, where library instruction is concerned with no more than one or two research tools at a time, the lesson should be geared to a specific topic: Indians, Inventions, Colonial Life, Alaska, and the like.

In the early grades, teachers share with librarians the task of teaching students the parts of a book, the use of a dictionary or encyclopedia, and the arrangement of books in a library. Later, students are introduced to the card catalog and the relationship of the catalog to the arrangement of books. Specialized reference works—the almanac, the biographical dictionary, the atlas—are brought in as the occasion demands.

The trend seems to be away from teaching isolated skills (use of the encyclopedia, the card catalog, the *Reader's Guide*) as ends in themselves or organizing such instruction into regular courses of study. Library skills are considered to be one component in a broad complex of work-study disciplines, of which more than a hundred have been identified. The importance of teaching the skills of efficient study is acknowledged but, here again, it is a neglected area both in theory and in practice. Very little is known about the best way of teaching study skills. And teachers themselves have had very little formal training in building their own study habits. It may well be that the acquisition of such skills is an intensely personal matter and achieved largely by a process of trial and error.

Opinion polls conducted among young people reveal that the majority of them wish they knew how to study better. They complain of deficiencies in such skills as locating sources of information, distinguishing the relevant from the irrelevant and the essential from the less important, taking notes, making outlines, writing reports, and studying for a test. The evidence seems to be that unless

LIBRARY INSTRUCTION

students are given specific instruction in proper work habits during the early years of elementary school, they will not develop efficient study skills subsequently. For this reason, training in these skills should be part of a school-wide program, beginning as early in the grades as possible and not left to the whim of individual teachers.

This training might well begin with simple exercises that call for locating topic sentences in a paragraph or reducing a paragraph to a single original summary sentence. Students might then go on to summarizing a page or two in two or three sentences. Later, a chapter or an essay may be briefly outlined. Finally, they are ready to prepare an original report, involving the manipulation of a variety of materials. In other words, the acquisition of study skills should be a graduated sequence, culminating in high school with research activities that call for the exercise of all previously acquired habits.

The importance of teaching library skills as part of a research project cannot be over-emphasized. Unless students see a reason for mastering the skills taught, the instruction arouses little interest or enthusiasm. To be most effective, library instruction is geared to a specific problem which students are asked to solve. Only as much information as students need to carry out their assignment successfully is conveyed. The specialized tools of the librarian have no place in the ordinary library lesson.

One of the drawbacks in using commercially prepared films, filmstrips, and instruction manuals on the library is that their content does not generally coincide with a given assignment. Frequently the forms used in these teaching aids are at variance with local usage. Librarians disagree on the correct method of labelling the spines of fiction books and biographies, on author letters, call numbers, and on other technical aspects of library practice. The result is confusion, particularly on the part of young children.

Occasionally on the elementary level or in cases where knowledge of the library is seriously deficient, it is useful to utilize a strictly formal approach. If students are unfamiliar with the arrangement of books, for example, they may be brought to the library for basic instruction and a small job sheet requiring them to locate books on the shelves and in the catalog.

If students have had little or no experience with encyclopedias, elementary drill and practice in the use of guide words or letters on the spine may be the only formal instruction needed.

An enlarged diagram or picture of the set, with the lettering clearly visible, makes a convenient visual aid. The instruction is followed by simple assignments calling for consultation of the appropriate volumes. Teaching children the comparative merits or unique features of the various encyclopedias has no place in the school curriculum. It is meaningless and futile to burden children with the details that are taught in graduate or undergraduate library science courses. Children do not need to know which encyclopedias have indexes or study guides and which do not. They can better profit from a knowledge of the kind of information found in an encyclopedia and how the information is presented. And the most practical way of acquiring this knowledge is through well-planned exercises derived from units of classroom work.

The best possible approach to formal library instruction is one which carries over immediately to a specific class assignment. Even in an orientation period, when students are being introduced to the library for the first time, the lesson becomes much more meaningful if students know there will be an immediate follow-up. The simplest expedient in this situation is for the teacher to require students to select a book for their first book report. The librarian's task is now reduced to discussing with the students the types of books that will be acceptable, to exhibit examples of such books, and to help students determine how such books are located in the library.

A singularly effective library period is one in which a class utilizes the library as a laboratory or workshop. In this case, a brief explanation by the librarian is followed by immediate access to the materials described. The use of the school library in this way is an educationally sound procedure often overlooked by teachers. It is especially feasible in libraries which have facilities to accommodate an entire class, either in an adjoining classroom or a separate alcove. In other cases, some compromise has to be effected, either clearing one area of the library for the class or trucking materials to the room where the class usually meets.

The library-laboratory method is particularly effective when a broad unit of work can easily be separated into smaller areas of concentration. Here, as an example, is how one such workshop arrangement was brought about. A teacher scanning the shelves for a suitable volume on urban problems finally selected Richard Whalen's *A City Destroying Itself* (Morrow, 1965) and brought it to the librarian.

LIBRARY INSTRUCTION

"Is this book available in paperback?" he asked. "I can check," was the librarian's response, "but why do you ask?" The teacher replied that he was about to undertake the study of cities in his social studies class and was looking for an inexpensive publication on the subject which all the students could purchase as a text. After some discussion with the librarian, he dropped the idea and agreed instead to try the librarian's suggestion for a workshop period. He divided the class into committees, making each committee responsible for investigating one phase of the unit. The topics selected for research were 1) housing and slum clearance 2) police power 3) education in ghetto schools 4) air and water pollution 5) social welfare problems and 6) the roots of violence. There was enough material on all of the topics to occupy the class for several periods of research and discussion.

When a class is scheduled for a period of laboratory work in the library, both teacher and librarian share in the necessary pre-liminaries. Prior consultation between the two confirms that space will be available and sufficient materials on hand for the entire group. It is the teacher's responsibility to see that students understand the assignment before undertaking to carry it out. It is disastrous to ask students to do research on "the rise of nationalist states," if they do not know what states (i.e. countries) are involved, the historical period covered, or the meaning of the term "nationalist."

When the class has gathered in the library, a few helpful hints by the librarian reduce fruitless searching. The nature of the materials to be used and their disposition in the library are made clear. During the period, the librarian helps individual students to find pertinent sources. The teacher is available to assist in interpretation. Verbatim copying is prevented. Once the students have settled down to skim and take notes, they are permitted to concentrate without interruption. Routine announcements, the collection of papers, or reminders of the next day's homework are avoided.

The use of the library as a workshop is particularly recommended in schools where rigid scheduling does not give students free time to visit the library, if they feel so inclined. The traditional study period, when students would normally have the option of the library or the study hall, has become such an administrative nuisance that many schools have eliminated it completely. The study hall, where there is one, is frequently in the auditorium, one of the least favorable environments for serious work. It lacks writing space, reference facilities, and able human guidance. The lighting is poor and supervision is troublesome. The problem does not exist in those favored schools where an independent study program guarantees free access to the library at almost any time.

At times the librarian is called upon to conduct a full-scale briefing to prepare the class for a long-term project. In this case it is incumbent upon him to prepare carefully. Much of his reputation among students derives from superior teaching of this kind. Consequently, he plans carefully and conducts the lesson in a professional manner. Questions are well-phrased and stimulating. If necessary, the key questions that will be asked are written out beforehand, even if they are not referred to in the course of the lesson. It is not always possible to predict the direction a lesson will take, but a set of fixed questions prepared in advance will help preserve the unity of the lesson.

Basically, the library lesson is a demonstration and dialogue. The demonstration consists of showing students examples of the materials they will use for their projects. The dialogue is a discussion between the students and the librarian during which all of the problems relating to the location of the materials are anticipated and analyzed. Illustrative materials are introduced into every library lesson. They hold the attention of students, arouse their curiosity, and serve as vehicles for the discussion which follows.

In preparing for the lesson, the librarian puts himself in the student's place and asks himself: "How would I go about doing this assignment?" The answers to this question constitute the lesson outline and assist in the selection of the materials that will be introduced to the class. The heart of the lesson is a series of questions designed to stimulate thinking and response on the part of as many pupils as possible. In the questioning close attention is paid to the key words (i.e. subject headings) under which students will search for the needed material. The first broad question is: What are the different kinds of books (or other materials) which might contain the desired information? As correct answers are given, examples are shown to the class. The second (and most important) question is: Under what key words will these books be found?

Assume that a class has reached the study of the medieval period in European history. The students have been asked to investigate aspects of life in the Middle Ages. In the briefing session, they are asked to nominate the kinds of books that should be examined: histories of Europe, histories of the Middle Ages, books about life in the medieval period, and histories of individual countries. They then proceed to suggest appropriate key words under which the books will be found listed in the catalog: FEUDALISM; KNIGHT-HOOD; CHIVALRY; MIDDLE AGES; EUROPE—HISTORY; MEDI-EVAL HISTORY; HISTORY, MEDIEVAL; ENGLAND—HISTORY; FRANCE—HISTORY; etc.

The same technique is applied where emphasis in the lesson is on the use of the *Readers' Guide*. A teacher asks his students to prepare brief persuasive speeches on topics of current interest. He presents the librarian with a list of the topics the students have selected and schedules a briefing session. The librarian assembles representative pamphlets, periodical articles, and books which the students will want to use. He begins the library lesson by asking the class to suggest procedures that have already been followed or that might be followed. There is a brief review of the library's method of handling pamphlets and of locating relevant material in books. Sample entries from the *Readers' Guide* are decoded. There follows intensive drill on naming all the possible subject entries that might apply to each of the topics. The topic of regulating the sale of firearms yields such suggestions as **weapons, guns, rifles,** and **firearms**. The topic of smoking is researched under **tobacco, smoking, cancer, lung cancer, cigarettes** and others. Material on the war against poverty elicits suggestions like **poverty, poor, slums, anti-poverty programs, unemployment** and the names of specific agencies or programs.

The problem of determining the correct key word in library research receives much more attention in the upper grades than with younger pupils. By the time students are in high school, they hopefully are familiar with the fundamentals of using a library and should need only a refinement of the techniques applicable to a given assignment. Drill in naming as many key entries for the topics assigned is one way of enhancing the value of a library lesson. This procedure is especially valuable when the research centers on such abstractions as: Should witnesses to a crime get involved? or Is violence justified in protesting an immoral war?

Some attention is also given to the specific aids contained in the various indexes to assist the reader in arriving at the correct entry. The question is put: What helps does the *Readers' Guide* (or other index) use to direct the reader to the proper key words? The answer is **see** and **see also** cross-references and sub-heads. This step leads naturally into the final phase of the lesson. The question is put: In using the cumulated issues of the *Readers' Guide,* you will find many articles listed. How do you select those which might prove most helpful? The answers from the class should bring out these facts: 1) Clues to the contents of an article may be derived from the wording of its title. 2) The length of the article may be a criterion. 3) The type of magazine may be a deciding factor. 4) The availability of the magazine (does the library have it?) is important.

In discussing the use of the card catalog for a given assignment, a similar summary is made. All feasible subject headings are nailed down. A series of cards with the correct headings is exhibited. The cards may be samples enlarged on illustrators' board or an overhead projector may be used. Questions then take this form: "What are the titles of these books? Which of them would you assume to be the most useful for this assignment? Why? What steps would you take to locate these books and others like them in the library? How would you determine whether the books actually contained the information you need? How would you go about abstracting this information? How would you list this book in a bibliography?

To reiterate, a major stumbling block to students in their search for information is failure to ascertain the correct entry under which to look. The inconsistency in the various tools of research does not make it any easier. The *New York Times Index* uses DRUG ADDICTION but the *Readers' Guide* prefers NARCOTIC HABIT. On the subject of prayers in the schools the *Readers' Guide* uses PUBLIC SCHOOLS AND RELIGION. The *New York Times Index* entry for this topic is RELIGIOUS PRACTICES IN PUBLIC SCHOOLS, ISSUE OF. A student using the *World Book Encyclopedia* for information on PIGS is referred to the article on HOGS, while *Collier's Encyclopedia* advises: PIGS see SWINE.

To help librarians and other information specialists standardize their indexing procedures, the *New York Times* has placed on the market a *Thesaurus of Descriptors.* This work is a large, loose-leaf, computer print-out (selling for $225.00) which suggests and defines specific subject headings and related headings. An advertisement for the thesaurus claims that, if five librarians were asked where they would file material on the "brain drain," the result would be five different answers. The thesaurus eliminates the guesswork by advising indexers to put such material under

IMMIGRATION—SCIENTIFIC AND TECHNICAL PERSONNEL

Parenthetically it may be observed that the problem of the key term is a major obstacle in the storage and retrieval of information in computerized centers. Before any data can be stored in machine-readable form, someone must decide on the proper catch-words under which the information will eventually be searched. At the National Library of Medicine, in Bethesda, Maryland, six experienced lexicographers and two non-professionals are employed for the sole purpose of keeping up-to-date a master list of medical subject headings (MeSH). This technical vocabulary list is the basis on which a large scale computerized system for the storage and retrieval of medical information (MEDLARS) depends.

Some systems avoid the key word problem altogether, by listing an article or a report under all the words in its title. Thus, a document on cosmic rays in outer space is listed under all the main words in its title and appears in the index in four places:

COSMIC RAYS IN OUTER SPACE
RAYS IN OUTER SPACE, COSMIC
OUTER SPACE, COSMIC RAYS IN
SPACE, COSMIC RAYS IN OUTER

It will be a long time before this KWIC (Key Word in Context) system or any other computerized method of information retrieval becomes available to students. It is also doubtful whether any system will ever eliminate completely the manual searching of information through printed indexes. Certainly students will continue to need instruction and practice in this procedure for both personal and professional satisfaction.

10

The Library in Action

The essential purpose of the school library/materials center (if it has not been made clear by now) is to help students find the media and information which they need to carry out classroom assignments and to satisfy their own personal interests. The librarian also works with teachers to enrich the program of instruction through supplementary (library) materials of every description. He provides the necessary materials and organizes them for efficient use. He teaches students what the materials are, where they are, and how they are used.

Above all, the library exists for the benefit of students. Nothing a librarian does, administratively or otherwise, interferes with close personal assistance to students. Attention to student needs is his primary obligation. He spends as little time as possible in his office or workroom and is rarely seen behind the charging desk. Clerical and housekeeping chores are performed by student aides or non-professionals.

In a modern school library, the work of the librarian has become exceedingly complex. If the school library continues along the lines it is now taking (as described earlier), the time will shortly arrive when a corps of specialists will be needed to staff the library properly. The head librarian will function as a department chairman, planning the work of the library, setting policy, assigning duties, and meeting with the other chairmen. One librarian will be involved in the selection and acquisition of material. Another will be part of a teaching team, coordinating library instruction with class projects. Still another will have the responsibility of the school's audio-visual program. Non-professional assistants will do all of the chores relating to the processing and circulation of materials and the monitoring of students. Today's librarian attempts to do the work of all these specialists. The task is almost beyond the capabilities of any one person.

Even in a traditional school setting, where the librarian deals only in printed materials, the demands on his time and competence leave little opportunity for the examination of materials or a leisurely contact with students. Yet the librarian must be ready and able to put his hands on just the right book or source of information at the time requested whatever the nature of the student's request. For the question "Do you have anything on Zen and Existentialism?" he must recall at once the excellent chapters in Abraham Kaplan's *New World of Philosophy.* If the student asks for "something on extrasensory perception," the librarian will reach for the section in John Mann's *Frontiers of Psychology.* If the request is for a comparison of the treatment of Caesar in Shakespeare and Plutarch, the student will be directed to a good annotated edition of the play. The demand for material on "the commercial revolution" will bring to mind the Anvil edition of H.L. Adelson's *Medieval Commerce* and a section in T.W. Wallbank's *Man's Story* (Scott, Foresman, 1964).

The librarian in a typical high school or college spends a large part of his working day in helping individual students with problems of this nature. Indeed, this one-to-one relationship is one of the more gratifying aspects of his job. The problems may have developed out of classroom situations, textbook assignments, or the personal needs of the students themselves.

Many of the questions are routine and require only a quick reference to some obvious source of information: Who said "No man is an islande"? Are "cumulative" and "accumulative" synonyms? What does "alienation" mean? What are the provisions of the twenty-sixth amendment? Has the amendment passed? What are the five postulates of Euclid? Do you have any poems by Allen Ginsberg?

Others are research topics designed to supplement a superficial textbook: Education in Soviet Russia, Science in Nazi Germany, the Arab Refugee Problem, Apartheid, Aid to Communist Countries, African Nationalism, Recognition of Red China, Overpopulation, the Alliance for Progress. Or they may be controversial items proposed by the teacher as a change of pace and to stimulate debate: Narcotics, Pollution, Flying Objects, the Assassination of President Kennedy, Sex Education, Vietnam, Alcoholism, Automobile Safety, Capital

THE LIBRARY IN ACTION

Punishment, Civil Disobedience, Teen Age Morality, Dropouts, Smoking, Censorship, Wiretapping, and the Invasion of Privacy.

On occasion the school librarian serves as more than a mere information consultant in these face-to-face confrontations with students. He is regarded as an adult of some wisdom and understanding who—unlike a parent, teacher, or a counselor—can take an objective stand and remain comparatively impartial. For example: A student buttonholes the librarian and asks "Why does a kid have to stay in school if he doesn't want to? Why can't he go out and get a job?" This student is asking for something more than a magazine article pro and con compulsory education or statistics on the fate of school dropouts. He is looking for an individual who will take time out to argue the case with him on a mature level and help him arrive at a satisfactory position.

Another student waits for a momentary lull in the library's proceedings before approaching the librarian. He is an honors student with an academic standing at the top of his class. Yet he is dissatisfied with the length of time it takes him to complete a reading assignment. Would a speed-reading course be of any value? Here again, no book on reading improvement or reading dynamics will satisfy the student. He is asking for a frank and knowledgeable opinion from an expert.

This incident introduces another sphere of activity for the school librarian—that of reading guidance. A student has seen a television play called *Sweet Potato Pie* and wants to read the book. Does the library have a copy? A check of the card catalog and *Books in Print* reveals that no such book can be found. When the student finishes telling about the play, the librarian says "I have something you may like. Here is the story of a young school teacher who was subjected to the vilest attacks because in Connecticut in 1827 she dared to admit a Negro child to her school. It is called *Prudence Crandall, Woman of Courage*. Are you interested?" The reaction is immediate: "That's for me!"

Another girl has graduated from the Du Jardin, Emery and Cavanna stage. She wants something similar to read but is tired of the empty, going steady, double date diet. Is there anything with a little more "bite"? The librarian suggests the *Rock and the Willow* (Lee), *Birch Interval* (Crawford), *Up a Road Slowly* (Allen), a *Question of Harmony* (Sprague).

A bright youngster has read Cather, Conrad, Lewis, Maugham and Steinbeck and wishes something on a more sophisticated level.

THE SCHOOL LIBRARY AND EDUCATIONAL CHANGE

The librarian suggests Camus, Virginia Woolf, Kafka, Mary Renault. Minutes later a reader at the other end of the ability scale arrives from the classroom with a note from the teacher: "Please give this boy something he can read." The librarian reaches for Bonham's *Durango Street.* "Would you like this story about a young fellow who returns from reform school determined to keep out of trouble but finds he must rejoin his old gang just for self-protection?" Sold.

Work with individual students who have reading problems is a far more exacting task than that of directing them to sources of information. It calls for a knowledge of books acquired from long and constant reading. It is an area too often handled with indifference because of the special skills required and the pressure of other routines. Yet the need to interest students in reading is paramount.

Assistance to teachers is another integral part of the librarian's daily schedule. A teacher who wishes to go beyond the range of the textbook seeks the librarian's help. Can a library unit (lesson and research) be constructed around various phases of some subject only casually treated in the text? Ideas are exchanged and a decision reached. Each student will take an incident or period in American history and examine it from the point of view of its treatment in fiction and non-fiction sources. A bibliography is requested to provide students with suggested references and an appointment made for a class briefing.

Another teacher has asked his classes to investigate and make a comparison of Russia and China or of Alexander the Great and Hitler or of Confucius and Mao Tse-tung. This time the librarian seeks out the teacher, gently remarking that students are having difficulty in finding and understanding suitable source material. He asks "Have you ever given this assignment before?" "To tell the truth," the teacher replies, "this is my first year of teaching. Can you give me any ideas?" The librarian says: "You say you are about to take up the study of India. Why not ask individual students to report on the various problems faced by that country: overpopulation, illiteracy, the caste system, religious frictions, economic weaknesses, health, relations with China and the like? Then do the same with other units of work." The idea takes hold and is successfully implemented.

The guidance counselor consults with the librarian. He is concerned because the school curriculum provides no opportunity for students to learn about career opportunities. He does not expect students to settle on a specific field of work at this point but he feels that they should begin to think about the problem. Can the library help? The librarian suggests that the chairman of English be called in for a three-way conference. The result is an assignment for all students in a given grade of English. Students will be asked to investigate any career field, describe the variety of jobs available in it, the personal and educational requirements of each, and the outlook for future employment. One purpose of the assignment is to expose students to the variety of career materials in the library—books, pamphlets, and reference sources. Another is to emphasize the changing nature of the job market and the broad range of opportunities available. A library lesson precedes the written work and introduces students to the sources they will need to use.

A teacher is puzzled. His students have just read several essays in a biography anthology. Can the librarian suggest a suitable follow-up for this unit? A number of possibilities are proposed. Perhaps the students can select a full-length book about some person of their own choosing—a hero they admire or someone who has succeeded in a career they are considering. Or a research assignment can be arranged involving the use of basic biographical research tools. In either case students will write a brief biographical account, similar in format to one of the essays read in class.

While these conferences are in progress, the normal routines of the library are carried on almost automatically. A corps of student aides has been trained to perform these chores without the need for close supervision. Materials are borrowed and returned with smooth efficiency. The tables are cleared of books and magazines left by previous readers. Periodicals are secured for students working on special reports. Shelves are straightened. New books are processed for circulation and old ones repaired or readied for re-binding. Traffic in and out of the library is controlled with minimum interference. All of these operations, seemingly effortless, are the result of careful training and an insistence on high level accuracy. In more fortunate schools, paraprofessionals, clerks, or secretaries supervise or take care of these routines.

One of the librarian's most sensitive areas of operation is the proper selection of materials from a vast output of current publications as well as an imposing backlist. Few people are aware of the amount of time which must be spent (most often outside of regular working hours) in choosing the titles most appropriate and essential to the individual library. Discriminating criteria are applied to each item. The reading interests and abilities of the student body are kept in mind. The librarian must be alert to changing demands and shifts in curriculum emphasis. He must be aware of gaps in the collection and be ready to defend his purchases in case of dispute.

If the library goes in heavily for paperbacks, as it should, the problem of selection is aggravated, for the list of books in this format is a staggering one. Pamphlets and government documents further compound the job of complete and careful selection. Of course, the librarian is assisted in the process of selection by professional journals and other book reviewing media. Teachers are also encouraged to make suggestions and should do so without being urged.

It is imperative that school librarians be given complete freedom in selection. Communities which restrict the librarian's purchases to state or locally-approved lists do a disservice to students. The requirement that books be supplied by a certified jobber is also a hindrance. Librarians must have the prerogative to act immediately on a recommendation for purchase, for it is in this way that readers are gained and reading encouraged. Moreover the demand in school libraries is in large part for current books and materials. An informal survey in one school library showed that more than fifty percent of the daily circulation consisted of books acquired during the preceding year. It has also been observed that the life of a book is in the first year after publication, after which it begins to gather dust. For these reasons, librarians in every type of library must be in a position to supply new books immediately upon publication, or even pre-publication if the need arises.

Once the books have arrived, the invoices checked, and payment approved, there is the technical job of getting the books ready for circulation as quickly as possible. The mechanical operations of stamping and pasting are no problem. They are done by student or non-professional help speedily and efficiently. The intellectual processes associated with the proper recording of the book's availability are another matter. The assignment of the correct classification number and the most suitable subject headings can be troublesome.

How, for example, should a book like Jack Newfield's *A Prophetic Minority* be entered in the catalog so as not to be missed by a student searching for information on dissident campus groups?

THE LIBRARY IN ACTION

Is the subject heading usually assigned to such books—RIGHT AND LEFT (POLITICAL SCIENCE)—a good one? Would students turn naturally to this heading? Or would NEW LEFT be a better choice? or RADICALISM? or STUDENT REVOLT? or SOCIAL DISSENT? Where in the catalog should a book on the draft be listed? Under DRAFT? MILITARY SERVICE? CONSCRIPTION? SELECTIVE SERVICE? ARMED FORCES? COMPULSORY MILITARY TRAINING?

What of a book like William Saroyan's *Look at Us; Let's See; Here We Are . . .,* a collection of photographs and accompanying text? Should it be classified and placed on the shelf in 917.3 (U.S. Civilization) or 973.91 (Twentieth Century America) or 778 (Photographic Essays) or 818 (American Miscellany)? Is the book *Scientists Who Work with Cameras* by Lynn Poole best shelved with collective biography (920) or in science (509) or with vocational guidance (371.3) or with the other books on photography (770)? These are just a few examples of cataloging and classification problems which require time for consideration and decision.

In recent years, great progress has been made in the commercial processing and cataloging of new books, in the conviction that individual librarians should be relieved of this chore. Librarians have for a long time had the option of purchasing printed catalog cards for most of the books they acquired either from the Library of Congress or the H. W. Wilson Company. More recently, a number of firms have gone into the business of securing books for libraries, providing the catalog cards, and shipping the books all prepared with plastic covers, call number labels, book pockets and cards, ready for immediate circulation. The future of this industry is a matter for conjecture but the market has already become a competitive one.

Some states or small governmental units are establishing regional processing and cataloging centers of their own to provide this service for school and public libraries. This undertaking is also a new development. While the time saving for the individual librarian is enormous under either plan, there still remains the difficulty of adjusting variant terms and format to local practices. But this problem is not insurmountable. A more serious drawback is the time lag between the time of ordering and the time of receipt. Books needed promptly will still require individual treatment. However, the idea of pre-processed and pre-cataloged books is well worth advancing, for the time of the librarian is better utilized in face-to-face service to individuals and groups.

THE SCHOOL LIBRARY AND EDUCATIONAL CHANGE

Now that the books are on the shelves and ready for circulation, the librarian undertakes an intensive campaign to get them in the hands of readers. By direct or subtle methods, he advertises their availability. Hall displays and library exhibits promote their presence. Lists of recent acquisitions, as skillfully and attractively prepared as possible, are sent to the classrooms at regular intervals. Casual comments are made to those browsing at the shelves or displays.

An effective job of promotion requires an intimate knowledge of the book itself. The librarian must therefore read constantly. He cannot convey the spirit or content of any book with honesty except from first-hand knowledge. Students are impatient with vague or superficial answers when they are prompted to ask about specific titles.

Finally, there is the all-consuming task of teaching students what materials are available in a library and how they may be located. Teachers from abroad sometimes question the need for such instruction. They are accustomed to taking classes to the library without fanfare and permitting them to browse or ferret out information without formal preliminaries. This procedure may be feasible in small, comparatively uncomplicated libraries. But modern school libraries have extensive collections and specialized resources which may be baffling to students. Suitable instruction saves time and temper on the part of teacher, pupil and librarian.

11

Keys to the Collection

BOOKS

The strength of any library is its circulating book collection. It is here that students can find books for private pleasure reading and those which clarify or give added dimension to the school curriculum. In high school libraries, the fiction section includes representative modern authors, both American and European, the standard authors of the nineteenth century, and a plethora of light fiction: mystery, spy, detective, adventure, humor, and sports. It is strong in historical fiction and provides social problem novels on adult themes and on an adult level. For the intermediate reader, it offers stories of romance and family and school stories. In libraries on the elementary level, there are picture books, easy books, and books for those who have learned to read independently.

Among the biographies are the lives of famous scientists and inventors who have contributed to man's understanding and well-being. There are the heroes of history from ancient times to the present. There are figures from the world of sport and entertainment. Famous authors are liberally represented and increasingly such works as Claude Brown's *Manchild in the Promised Land* (Macmillan, 1965), the *Autobiography of Malcolm X* (Grove, 1967), and Ann Moody's *Coming of Age in Mississippi* (Dial, 1968) for the senior high school reader seeking insights into the Black Experience.

The non-fiction books are primarily a source of enrichment for the various courses taught in the school. Popular treatments of history, mathematics, science, and the social studies make difficult subjects more intelligible and stimulate curiosity. The 800's section contains a plentiful supply of plays and poetry and offers surveys of literature in its various forms, including criticisms of notable authors. There is an abundance of books on individual sports, a strong art section, handbooks on automobile driving and repair, and (for the girls) domestic arts and fashion. The librarian, alert to fads among the young, buys in accordance with the latest trends. At the moment, books on rock music, zen philosophy, mysticism, avant garde poetry, and the film are enjoying great popularity. Books on sex education, drug addiction, and the student rebellion are in demand.

There are numerous guides to the book resources of the school library. The basic bibliographies are those which have been prepared and kept up to date by the H. W. Wilson Company and the American Library Association. Wilson's *Senior High School Library Catalog* (formerly called the *Standard Catalog for High School Libraries)* is a list of books recommended for initial purchase by high schools. The list is revised every five years, with supplements published annually. The latest (9th) edition, issued in 1967, contains 4,231 recommendations for grades ten through twelve. The titles are arranged in library shelf order (Dewey Decimal classification) and each is carefully annotated. A detailed subject, title, and author index, with many analytics (parts of books), is provided.

The *Catalog* has been criticized as being too meagre in the light of increasing student needs and rapidly expanding school libraries but it should be regarded as a core list only. The *Junior High School Library Catalog* (2d edition, 1970), with 3,411 books recommended and four annual supplements (1971-1974) performs the same service for libraries in intermediate schools, grades seven through nine. *4000 Books for Secondary School Libraries* (Bowker, 1966) will be superseded in 1971 by *Books for Secondary School Libraries, a Basic List,* compiled by the Library Committee of the National Association of Independent Schools. It will recommend about 5,000 books and a scattering of non-book materials suitable for college-bound high school students.

The American Library Association's comparable (but smaller) compilations are the *Basic Book Collection for High Schools* (7th edition, 1963), with 1,700 titles and 70 periodicals recommended, and the *Basic Book Collection for Junior High Schools* (3d edition, 1960) with 1,000 titles and 70 magazines. Equivalent publications

KEYS TO THE COLLECTION

for the elementary school are *Books for Elementary School Libraries, an Initial Collection* by Elizabeth D. Hodges (American Library Association, 1969), with approximately 3,080 books representing a first-purchase, first-year collection for new schools. The latest edition of the *Children's Catalog* (Wilson, 1971) suggests 4,274 titles for elementary school readers.

The Elementary School Library Collection: a Guide to Books and Other Media, Phases 1-2-3, 5th Edition, edited by Mary Ann Gaver (Bro-Dart Foundation, 1970) is a much more comprehensive work. It is to date the most complete single listing of books and non-book media for the elementary school library program. 8,000 books and 2,000 audio-visual materials have been grouped into six categories (reference, non-fiction, fiction, easy books, periodicals, and professional tools). The term Phase 1, 2, or 3 applied to each item refers to its priority of acquisition as the library increases in strength. This work is an excellent example of a cross-media index.

As a special service to libraries on all levels, a number of commercial book wholesalers have prepared their own buying guides. Since these jobbers are in business primarily to sell books (processed, cataloged, and ready for immediate circulation), the coverage is naturally broader. The catalogs are available free. They are Bro-Dart's *Library Books for School and Public Libraries* (50,000 titles) and its supplement *Guide to Elementary School Library Books* (5,000 titles); Baker and Taylor's *Guide to the Selection of Books for Your Secondary School Library* and *Guide to the Selection of Books for Your Elementary School Library* (about 10,000 titles in each); the catalogs of the American Library and Education Service Company—Alesco—(16,000 titles in their program and a Simplified Selection Guide); and the *Xerox Contemporary High School Library Program* (10,000 titles).

Of course, the key to the resources of the individual school library is its own card catalog. Some schools are experimenting with a computer-produced catalog in book form so that copies of the catalog can be consulted in various parts of the building and by several users simultaneously. However, the economy of this move is open to question and most school libraries are continuing with the traditional catalog on cards. Rapidly growing and changing collections make the card catalog a more accurate tool and easier to keep up to date. The quality of the catalog—that is, its usefulness as a guide to the contents of the library—depends on the competence of the librarian responsible for it and the amount of time devoted to it.

THE SCHOOL LIBRARY AND EDUCATIONAL CHANGE

Some of the problems related to the making of a fool-proof catalog (particularly in the matter of subject entries) have been described in the previous chapter. In any event, the users of the catalog should be able without too much aimless searching to find answers to such questions as: What books (or other materials) does the library have on the subject of _____ ? What books does the library have by _____ ? Does the library have the book entitled _____ ? Where are these materials located?

The modern school library includes in its catalog not only the books in the library proper but also those which have been placed in supplementary resource centers (if any) dispersed throughout the building. It will also provide by means of color coded cards a listing of the films, filmstrips, recordings, tapes, and other non-print materials acquired for individual or group use.

On occasion requests come to the librarian for information about books not represented in the library's collection. For this purpose and for the librarian's own bibliographic needs, it is worthwhile to acquire from time to time the annual publications *Books in Print* and the *Subject Guide to Books in Print* (R.R. Bowker Co.). The 1968 edition of *Books in Print* was produced for the first time by computer and many gaps and errors appeared in it. However, the accuracy of later editions improved as expertise in computerized publishing developed.

Children's Books in Print is an annual author, title, and illustrator index of available (in print) books for children. Approximately 30,000 titles suitable for readers in grades kindergarten through twelve were listed in the first edition (Bowker, 1969) and 38,000 in the second (1970). A topical arrangement of those titles classifiable by subject (almost 8,000 headings) is provided by the companion volume *Subject Guide to Children's Books in Print* (Bowker, 1971).

The *Cumulative Book Index* published at intervals during the year and cumulated from time to time is an author, title, subject, and series record of all books in English published in the United States and some from abroad. The CBI is a supplement to the large basic volume: *The United States Catalog: Books in Print Jan. 1, 1928.* These indexes provide precise bibliographic data for every book listed: author's full name, complete title, year of publication, number of pages, publisher, and price.

A valuable adjunct is the *Book Review Digest* which excerpts reviews of hardbound fiction and non-fiction books from approximately seventy-five reviewing periodicals. A subject-title index at the back of each issue enhances the value of the set, which consists of annual bound volumes plus the current numbers.

The first edition of *The Bookman's Manual* was published by Bowker in 1921 as an aid to booksellers in the choice of titles and editions. Renamed *The Reader's Adviser,* this superb work is now in its eleventh edition and expanded into two volumes. It is a mine of information about books, authors, and the literature of the individual subject areas. Five thousand authors and 10,000 titles are represented. Volume One covers American and British fiction, poetry, drama, essays, and foreign literature. Volume Two deals with religion, folklore, humor, philosophy, science, psychology, history and other broad fields. The wealth of detail, including concise evaluations for each author and critiques for each genre, makes it an indispensable tool for librarians in secondary schools and colleges. The chapters on reference books (encyclopedias, atlases, and dictionaries) have been dropped as this information is now available in other sources.

Another excellent source of information about books, and one which has many uses in a high school library, is the *Guide to the Study of the United States of America,* prepared by staff members of the Library of Congress and published by the Government Printing Office in 1960. The purpose of this volume is to provide for students an annotated list of the important books about American civilization. Some of the subjects covered are literature, history (including intellectual, military, regional, and diplomatic), science, education, entertainment, art, law, and politics. The introductory statement at the head of each chapter and the descriptive notes for each author are models of discriminating judgment.

Students in every school should have at their disposal a tremendous choice of paperbound books. The paperbounds for recreational reading in high school will include most of the titles in the Berkley, Nova, Tempo, TAB, Lancer, Dell, and Pyramid series. For readers in elementary and middle schools, appropriate paperback titles are available in the Seafarer (Viking), Voyager (Harcourt), Camelot (Avon), Yearling (Dell), and Starline (Scholastic) editions. These books receive minimum processing and record keeping by the librarian (see page 66). They are exhibited for quick selection in strategically placed book racks, with replacements stored and brought out as needed. Their circulation is on the honor system, with losses taken for granted. The more expensive paperbound books (those in the Spectrum, Meridian, Torchbook, Vintage, Universal, and other editions) are treated as regular hardbound books, classified, cataloged, and shelved in the regular collection and sent for re-binding at the first sign of wear.

A complete listing of all books available in paper format is provided by *Paperbound Books in Print,* published three times a year by R.R. Bowker Company. Beginning in 1972, there will be only two semi-annual issues (July and November). This is the source which must be consulted to learn whether a specific title can be obtained in a paperback edition or what paperbacks are available on a given subject. The former practice of issuing monthly supplements (entitled *The Month Ahead*) was discontinued in 1971. The loss of this monthly service is unfortunate. Not only was it possible to obtain a preview of forthcoming titles (annotated) but the supplements contained carefully prepared essays and bibliographies on subjects of immediate interest to students and teachers (narcotics, black history, student unrest, urban deterioration, etc.).

The first edition of *Paperbound Books in Print* appeared in 1955 with a listing of 4,500 inexpensive reprints. Its present size (88,500 titles in March 1971) makes it a formidable selection tool for school libraries. However, much time is conserved if attention is concentrated on the section headed JUVENILES and other pertinent subject areas. The process of selection is further simplified if purchase is limited to the editions prepared specifically for young readers and mentioned previously. Additional assistance with this problem is rendered by subscription to the numerous book clubs organized for students in elementary and secondary schools. The Scholastic Book Clubs have programs for readers on five different levels and American Education Publications have three (primary, intermediate, and senior).

AUDIO-VISUAL MEDIA

There are, as yet, no evaluation services for non-print materials comparable to those for printed matter. Projected for the future is a federal network of media selection centers to be established by the National Book Committee and funded by the United States Office of

KEYS TO THE COLLECTION

Education. When the final phase (Phase IV) of the project is completed—the target date is 1978 or sooner—librarians, teachers, curriculum specialists, and other interested adults will have model collections to use in selecting all types of material for children of all ages and abilities. During the eighteen-month period of Phase I, 2,300 existing media centers were queried, 440 received follow-up questionnaires, and 50 were studied in depth in order to fashion a picture of current practices. The program is now in Phase II, during which a guide to objectives will be prepared and a set of principles for selection and acquisition will be formulated. Phases III and IV will see the establishment of the model centers and their evaluation.

In the meantime, librarians concerned with building multimedia collections must rely on a diversity of reviewing services. Previously it was possible to consult H.W. Wilson's *Educational Film Guide* (published between 1953 and 1962) and the *Filmstrip Guide* (1955-1962), but both of these tools have been discontinued. The second edition of *Guides to Newer Educational Media* by Margaret I. Rufsvold and Carolyn Guss (American Library Association, 1967) is a bibliography of sources for obtaining "films, filmstrips, kinescopes, phonodiscs, phonotapes, programmed instructional materials, slides, transparencies, videotapes." It describes the catalogs of audiovisual materials available from professional (not commercial) organizations and periodicals devoted to the newer educational media.

For a number of years the Educators Progress Service of Randolph, Wisconsin, has compiled annual listings of free material in non-print format. (Printed bulletins, pamphlets, and charts are sometimes included.) These are the *Educators Guide to Free Films,* the *Educators Guide to Free Filmstrips,* the *Educators Guide to Free Guidance Materials,* the *Educators Guide to Free Science Materials,* the *Educators Guide to Free Social Studies Material,* and the *Educators Guide to Free Tapes, Scripts, and Transcriptions.* The cost of these large paperbound volumes varies from $6.50 to $9.50. Most of the items listed are free for the asking; others (the films) are free on loan. The entries are annotated and instructions are given on how to use the items as well as how to obtain them.

In 1964 the McGraw-Hill Book Company published a fourteen volume *Educational Media Index* which was intended as a comprehensive guide to all available instructional media for every academic level on subjects ranging from agriculture to teacher education.

However, dissatisfaction with the EMI (which was prepared from computer copy) was evident soon after publication and distribution of the set was halted. In 1967 McGraw-Hill awarded a grant to the University of Southern California to add all the listings in EMI to its automated catalog of educational media and to provide a new edition of the EMI along with other catalogs.

The audio-visual bank at the University of Southern California (known as the National Information Center for Educational Media or NICEM) is reputed to be the largest of its kind in the world. The first of its projected commercial catalogs began to appear late in 1969 under the Bowker imprint. The same arrangement—twenty six broad subject areas and some four hundred subdivisions—is used in all four of these indexes. They are the *Index to 16mm Educational Films* (2d ed., 1969—almost 28,000 motion pictures listed); the *Index to Overhead Transparencies* (1969—17,000 items); the *Index to 8mm Motion Cartridges* (1969—8,900 sound and silent motion picture cartridges); and the *Index to 35mm Educational Filmstrips* (2d ed., 1970—approximately 25,000 filmstrips with and without sound). No new editions are planned for the future by the publisher but it is possible that the university or some other organization may decide to continue the revisions.

Some librarians report success in using the seven volume *Learning Directory 1970-71,* compiled by the Westinghouse Learning Corporation and designed as a guide to some 200,000 different print and non-print materials, including microforms, charts, periodicals, globes, maps, games, and other equipment. For data on multi-media products, distributors, review services, and audio-visual statistics, workers in this area refer to Bowker's *Audio-Visual Market Place, a Multi-media Guide* (2d ed., 1970).

The Booklist of the American Library Association (a semi-monthly book buying guide for librarians) began reviewing audio-visual material in the fall of 1969. The latest available issue contains evaluations of 16mm films, 8mm film loops, filmstrips, and non-musical recordings. Inclusion of an item in *The Booklist* constitutes approval for purchase. The critical comments are by qualified groups and indicate grade level and suggested curriculum placement.

The monthly *School Library Journal,* published separately or as part of the semi-monthly *Library Journal,* provides a similar service in its columns headed "Recordings," "Screenings," and "Media

Mix." Included in the last grouping are prints, slides, transparencies, and kits. Evaluations are by individuals and signed. A semi-annual "SLJ Audio-Visual Guide: a Multi-Media Subject List" in the same periodical provides information on forthcoming films, loops, filmstrips, academic games, and other learning materials in non-print format.

Other sources of information concerning new non-print products are the periodicals in the field *(Audio-Visual Instruction, Educational Technology, Educational Product Report, Educational Screen and A-V Guide, Film News)*, all of which carry information about new products and releases. A more complete survey of audio-visual selection aids (along with detailed instructions on their acquisition, organization, and circulation) is contained in *Developing Multi-Media Libraries* by Warren B. Hicks and Alma May Tillin which was published by Bowker in 1970.

CURRENT INFORMATION

There is no substitute for the school library's magazine collection as a source of information on problems of current interest and as a source of pleasure for casual browsers and special interest buffs. The collection will include magazines of general interest, some of genuine literary merit, a few scholarly periodicals, journals of contemporary history, and many periodicals of particular appeal to young people and hobbyists. Teachers should be familiar with those in their own subject fields and be able to direct students to noteworthy articles.

Current issues of all magazines received are made directly accessible in the library's reading room. Back issues are kept readily available in the reference or stack area. They are retained for a period of time determined by the librarian. Five years is a good average for weeklies and ten years for monthlies. The amount of storage space is naturally a determining factor.

The binding of magazines is generally not recommended for school libraries, since their chief value is their immediacy. A more desirable investment is the purchase on microfilm of those periodicals most frequently requested for research purposes. The investment is an economical one and the saving of storage space considerable. The microfilm edition, however, has two disadvantages. A volume can be consulted by only one person at a time and it cannot be borrowed for home use, since a viewer is needed to make the film readable. Well-endowed libraries may want to purchase a microfilm reader-printer which permits the reader to reproduce the pages needed for use outside the library.

The standard guide to the contents of periodicals is the *Readers' Guide to Periodical Literature.* Every teacher and every student should be thoroughly familiar with the use of this indispensable tool. The *Readers' Guide* serves as an index to approximately 158 of the most popular magazines published in this country. The list of magazines indexed, which appears in the front of each issue, varies from time to time in accordance with recommendations made from a poll of practicing librarians. The *Readers' Guide* appears twice a month (once in July and once in August) and the issues are cumulated according to an established publication schedule. Until 1966 the *Guide* was cumulated into biennial bound volumes. Since then the largest cumulation has been the annual.

The *Readers' Guide* provides an author and subject listing. For each article included it gives the name of the author (when known), the title of the article, the name of the magazine, its date, and the pages on which the article appears. Many abbreviations are used in the interest of space conservation and the key to abbreviations must be consulted in cases of doubt. Certain features of the *Guide* are worth noting, namely the listings for reviews of motion pictures (under MOVING PICTURE PLAYS—Criticisms, plots, etc.) and of plays (under DRAMA—Criticisms, plots, etc.).

Small libraries may subscribe to the *Abridged Readers' Guide* which is structured in the same way as the parent set but which indexes fewer magazines (about forty). The feeling is that it is simpler to use and more economical for schools on the lower level. In other cases, however, the popularity and value of the library's periodical collection make the regular *Readers' Guide* a better buy.

The *Readers' Guide to Periodical Literature* and the *Abridged Readers' Guide* are only two of many similar periodical indexes published by the Wilson company. Of particular importance to subject specialists are the *Education Index,* the *Art Index,* the *Social Science and Humanities Index* (until 1965 this work was called the *International Index*), the *Business Periodicals Index,* the *Biological and Agricultural Index,* and the *Applied Science and Technology Index* (formerly entitled the *Industrial Arts Index*). All are structured in the same way as the *Readers' Guide* but they index specialized journals rather than periodicals of general interest. Except for the *Education Index,* they are not normally received by school libraries but teachers ought to know about them.

The list of periodicals indexed which appears in the front of each issue of the *Readers' Guide* serves as a basic selection tool for the school librarian. Another excellent aid is *Periodicals for School Libraries, a Guide to Magazines, Newspapers, and Periodical Indexes,* compiled by a committee of the American Library Association under the direction of Marion H. Scott (American Library Association, 1969). The selection is a broad one, designed to meet the needs of all grade levels and a wide range of reader interests. There are full annotations for each periodical listed and a useful subject index.

School librarians who justifiably spend a large portion of their budgets for periodicals will benefit from a consultation of *Magazines for Libraries,* edited by Bill Katz (Bowker, 1969). It will help to answer such questions as: Which should I buy—*Coins* or *Coin World*? *Modern Screen* or *Films in Review*? Two thousand periodicals have been expertly evaluated in this outstanding volume. Each entry contains the essential bibliographic data (full title of magazine, year of original publication, frequency, name of editor, address, price, circulation figures, where indexed, and the number and length of book reviews carried) and full, critical descriptions. The main arrangement is alphabetical (from ACCOUNTING to WOMEN) with supplementary lists of free periodicals, underground newspapers, and other useful categories. Each magazine is rated as to its overall and reference value and its audience level. Browsing through this volume is an educational and entertaining experience. It is a superior selection tool as well as a rich source of detail for high school language arts classes studying the mass media.

The second edition of *From Radical Left to Extreme Right* edited by Robert H. Muller (Campus Publishers, Ann Arbor, 1970) summarizes by means of content samples the virtues and failings of some four hundred organs of persuasion. The periodicals are grouped into categories: Civil Rights, Racial and Ethnic Pride, Peace, and the like. Students and teachers developing magazine units for study will find this book another dependable source of information about magazines with a strong editorial bias.

A second source of information on topics of contemporary interest and for background on controversial issues is the library's

Information File. This resource contains the library's collection of pamphlets, documents, and clippings. Other methods of housing the pamphlets may be employed but the majority of school libraries find it convenient to place them alphabetically by subject into the folders of a Vertical (Information) File. Practical suggestions for organizing and maintaining an Information File are contained in *The Vertical File and Its Satellites, a Handbook of Acquisition, Processing, and Organization* (Libraries Unlimited, 1971). Sources of material for the Information File and methods of handling the material are described.

The pamphlet collection is assembled and replenished in several ways. Many leaflets, bulletins, and brochures arrive in the mail unsolicited and some are worth keeping. Others are selected deliberately from standard guides, such as H.W. Wilson's *Vertical File Index,* a monthly listing of free and low cost materials available from a variety of organizations. The *Public Affairs Information Service* (PAIS) is a weekly bibliographic bulletin which lists current books, articles, documents, and pamphlets in the social sciences but it is too specialized and costly for most school libraries.

Valuable additions to the school library's Information File come from the stream of documents emanating from various government agencies. Much time and patience is consumed in searching out those which are appropriate for student and teacher use. The semi-monthly bulletin issued by the Superintendent of Documents entitled *Selected United States Government Publications* provides some assistance in this area. Individuals and libraries can put themselves on the mailing list for this free and popular listing. The documents themselves are purchased by check or money order but acquisition is simplified if they are ordered by catalog number and the required number of document stamps is enclosed. The stamps are purchased in advance from the Superintendent of Documents for five cents each.

"Selected Government Publications" is a feature of the monthly *Wilson Library Bulletin.* This column reviews a dozen or more documents recommended for library purchase in each issue. A similar column appears intermittently in *The Booklist,* the American Library Association's semi-monthly buying guide. For a basic list of governmental documents which are of interest to the average consumer, the reader is referred to the paperback *Over 2000 Free Publications Yours for the Asking* compiled by Frederick J. O'Hara (New American Library, 1968).

KEYS TO THE COLLECTION

The bulk of the school library's pamphlet collection is made up of serial publications paid for on annual subscription. The *Public Affairs Pamphlets,* published by the Public Affairs Committee at monthly intervals, are devoted to subjects of public interest: crime, inflation, religion, law, health, and the social services. The Foreign Policy Association issues a new *Headline Book* every other month. This series is usually concerned with aspects of United States foreign policy. Recent numbers have dealt with France, Southeast Asia, Vietnam, Britain, India, and Eastern Europe. A four-page leaflet (and an excellent value for the money) is the monthly publication *Vital Issues,* prepared by the Center for Information on America of Washington, Connecticut. The leaflets are objective summaries of subjects like population change, natural and human resources, urban problems, and economic planning.

A more expensive but exceedingly valuable service for classes studying contemporary problems and developments is the weekly *Editorial Research Reports,* published by Congressional Quarterly of Washington, D.C. The reports average fifteen to twenty pages in length and present impartial studies of current affairs. Some of the topics that have been examined in recent issues are: community control, black pride, the peace movement, heart surgery, the credibility gap, Nigeria, human intelligence, communal living, the mass media, and chemical-biological warfare. The service includes semi-annual bound volumes containing duplicates of the reports and a five year subject-title index.

One or more subscriptions to the *American Observer* are an inexpensive and worthwhile acquisition for school libraries. Until recently it was published as a weekly newsletter for secondary school readers. Acquired in 1970 by Scholastic Magazines, Inc., it now appears bi-weekly (seventeen times) during the school year. Each issue is twenty-four pages in length, contains no advertising, and features several long articles on timely subjects written in a manner to spur critical thinking and further reading. Cartoons and other short items enliven the new format. While aimed toward classroom use, the *American Observer* will be useful in libraries and, if more than one copy is ordered, can provide a good source of cuttings for the Information File. Duplicate copies of *Senior Scholastic* (or its junior equivalent for intermediate schools) are another source of clippings geared to student needs and abilities, in particular the pro and con discussions of controversial issues.

THE SCHOOL LIBRARY AND EDUCATIONAL CHANGE

A subscription to the *New York Times* is an essential item for all libraries, except for those serving schools on the elementary level. Copies of the *Times* are kept on file for a brief period and important articles are subsequently excerpted for the Information File, if the need exists and time permits. School libraries also receive at least one local newspaper for items of community interest.

In schools where contemporary national and international problems are an important part of the curriculum, a file of the *New York Times* on microfilm is a valuable asset. The cost of an annual microfilm subscription along with the *New York Times Index* (without which access to the contents of the newspaper becomes impossible) is more than $400 but the purchase is mandatory if high quality reference service is to be given. A spool of the microfilm contains a ten-day to two-week run of the newspaper. The *Index* is a semi-monthly periodical, replaced annually by a bound volume. The mechanics of using the *Index* are complex (the cross-references are baffling to the average user) and students will need personal assistance with it. Group instruction is indicated when assignments require large numbers of students to make use of it.

REFERENCE BOOKS

Although the bulk of library research done by students is carried out through the library's circulating book collection and its file of current materials, standard reference works are needed for the occasional overview of a subject or quick answers to random questions. Any number of tools exist to aid the librarian in building a basic reference collection. Constance M. Winchell's *Guide to Reference Books* (8th ed., American Library Association, 1967) and its two supplements are probably too detailed for this purpose. Frances Neel Cheney's *Fundamental Reference Sources* (American Library Association, 1971) may be more practical for school libraries. In any case, one of these volumes should be on hand for questions from the faculty on the relative merits of a particular reference work or whether a primary source book exists in a given field.

School librarians will find some less ambitious guides helpful in making first purchase selections. Since 1938 the Enoch Pratt Free Library of Baltimore, Maryland, has been publishing a valuable

KEYS TO THE COLLECTION

handbook describing reference books recommended for small and medium-sized libraries. The current edition of *Reference Books, a Brief Guide* (7th ed., 1970) supplies critical comment on eight hundred and fifteen different titles. Even this number is too many for school libraries and judicious selection must be exercised.

Another possibility is *Reference Books for Small and Medium Sized Public Libraries,* compiled by the Basic Reference Committee of the American Library Association in 1969. This book is a descriptive list of important bibliographies, encyclopedias, and specialized works in religion, business, science, education, and other broad fields, It contains adult works only and is aimed toward newly established libraries or those wishing to strengthen existing collections. Librarians serving in intermediate and elementary schools may want to check Carolyn C. Peterson's *Reference Books for Elementary and Junior High School Libraries* (Scarecrow, 1970).

The *American Reference Books Annual,* published by Libraries Unlimited, Inc., is a new series designed to keep librarians informed of new tools for meeting reference needs. Publication began with the 1970 volume, which reviewed approximately 1,500 books published during 1969. The second (1971) annual reviewed 1,900 reference books published during 1970. The reviews are by subject specialists and are signed.

For an evaluation of encyclopedias, either as library acquisitions or as an investment by prospective individual buyers, the librarian refers to *General Encyclopedias in Print 1969, a Comparative Analysis* by S. Padraig Walsh (Bowker, 1969). This small work describes and analyzes thirty-seven encyclopedia sets published in the United States and seventeen other works of lesser importance. It combines advice on how to choose an encyclopedia with detailed information on the publishing history of each set, its scope, revision policy, physical make-up, and other attributes.

The same author has prepared a guide to other reference books in his *Home Reference Books in Print: Atlases, English Language Dictionaries and Subscription Books* (Bowker, 1969). A similar outline format is employed. In addition to helpful notes on dictionaries and atlases, this work describes such sets as *Great Books of the Western World* (56 volumes) and *Gateway to Great Books* (10 volumes) and other notable and some lesser known reference works.

TEACHERS' PROFESSIONAL COLLECTION

The 1969 *Standards for School Media Programs* advocates a professional library in each school building consisting of two hundred to a thousand volumes and forty to fifty professional journals. Books and periodicals on methodology, psychology, guidance, testing, classroom management, and educational reform form the core of this collection. Curriculum guides, teachers' manuals, publishers' catalogs, and indexes of community resources and of audio-visual materials are also a legitimate part of it. The aim is to up-grade teacher competence and to keep school personnel abreast of changes in educational thinking and practice.

Primary consideration is given to teacher recommendations in building the professional library. The collection is kept fresh and alive by the purchase of new items noted in the reviewing media. Several attempts have been made at compiling a suggested basic library for teachers but the results have not been overwhelmingly successful. *The Teachers' Library: How to Organize It and What to Include* (National Education Association, 1968) has some useful suggestions for purchase as well as recommendations for organizing and promoting the professional collection. Representatives from fifty-four organizations assisted in preparing the list of books, periodicals and films. Speech, music, science, health, industrial arts, and audio-visual education are some of the areas covered.

REFERENCES CITED

1. James S. Coleman. *The Equality of Educational Opportunity.* Washington, D.C., U.S. Government Printing Office, 1966.

2. J.I. Goodlad. "The Schools vs. Education", *Saturday Review,* April 19, 1969, p. 59.

3. Charles E. Silberman. "High Schools that Work", *Atlantic,* August 1970, p. 98.

4. Daniel N. Fader. "Attention Must Be Paid", *Wilson Library Bulletin,* Oct. 1968, pp. 146-151.

5. Quoted in Paul Monore, ed. *Cyclopedia of Education,* New York, Macmillan, 1912, vol. 4, p. 17.

6. Reprinted in Martha Wilson, ed. *Selected Articles on School Library Experience,* New York, Wilson, 1925, pp. 171-172.

7. M.G. Baxter and others. *The Teaching of American History in High Schools,* Bloomington, Ind., Indiana University Press, 1964.

8. J.E. Wiltz. *Books in American History.* Bloomington, Ind., Indiana University Press, 1964.

9. Paul Woodring. *Introduction to American Education.* New York, Harcourt, 1965, p. 21.

10. R.W. Taylor. "Forces Redirecting Science Teaching", *Science Teacher,* October, 1962. (Reprinted in Alfred de Grazia and David A. Sohn. *Revolution in Teaching: New Theory, Technology, and Curricula,* New York, Bantam, 1964, p. 191).

11. Neil Postman and Charles Weingartner. *Teaching as a Subversive Activity.* New York, Delacorte, 1969.

12. Figures from Ellsworth Mason. "Contemporary Education, a Double View", *Library Journal,* Nov. 15, 1969, pp. 4201-4206.

13. Reported in the *New York Times,* July 23, 1969, p. 28 and July 27, 1969, Sec. IV, p. 9.

14. *Children and Their Primary Schools.* 2 vol. London, His Majesty's Stationer's Office, 1967. (The Plowden Report).

15. William K. Stevens. "North Dakota Moves to Make Elementary Education Less Rigid", *New York Times,* Oct. 11, 1970, p. 68. Also, Charles E. Silberman. *Crisis in the Classroom,* New York, Random House, 1970, p. 284.

16. Reported in the *New York Times,* Feb. 13, 1970, p. 34. Also, Myron Brenton. "Breakaway Students Try Their Own Schools", *Think* (magazine), Sept.-Oct. 1970, p. 29-32.

17. B. Frank Brown. *The Nongraded High School.* Englewood Cliffs, N.J., Prentice-Hall, 1963.

18. Alvin Toffler. *Future Shock.* New York, Random House, 1970, Ch. 5

19. "Million Dollar Carrels", *Library Journal,* Jan. 15, 1967, pp. 306-310.

20. R. W. Locke. "Has the Education Industry Lost Its Nerve?", *Saturday Review,* Jan. 16, 1971, pp. 42-43.

21. Mary E. Hall. "The Development of the Modern High School Library", *Library Journal,* Sept. 1915, p. 627.

22. Chase Dane. "The Changing School Library: An Instructional Media Center" in Melvin J. Voigt. *Advances in Librarianship,* Vol. 1, New York, Academic Press, 1970, pp. 133-157.

23. From Robert G. Ames. "A Library's Role—Instructional Materials Center", Wisconsin Education Association, Dec. 1964. Reprinted in N.P. Pearson and Lucius Butler. *Instructional Materials Centers: Selected Readings.* Minneapolis, Minn., Burgess Pub. Co., 1969, pp. 128-130.

REFERENCES CITED

24. Henry J. Ford. "The Instructional Resources Center, an Enabling Facility", *Audiovisual Instruction,* Oct. 1962. Reprinted in Pearson and Butler, op. cit., pp. 136-140.

25. "Fifteen Little Indians", *New Republic,* June 17, 1967, p. 6.

26. Joseph Featherstone. "Classroom Gadgetry", *New Republic,* May 31, 1969, pp. 10-11.

27. Fred Hechinger. "Time to Teach Those Teaching Machines", *New York Times,* Feb. 8, 1970, Sec. IV, p. 9.

28. Sherman Williams. *School Libraries: Their History, Development, Present Purpose and Function in Our Educational System.* Albany, N.Y., New York State Education Department, 1922. (pamphlet)

29. L.C. Fay and A.T. Eaton. *Instruction in the Use of Books and Libraries,* Boston, Faxon, 1919; Margaret Hutchins. *Guide to the Use of Libraries,* New York, Wilson, 1920; and O.A. Rice. *Lessons on the Use of Books and Libraries.* Chicago, Rand McNally, 1920.

30. Budd L. Gambee. "Standards for School Media Programs, 1970; a Lesson from History", *American Libraries,* May 1970, pp. 483-485.

31. James Squire and R.K. Applebee. *High School English Instruction Today.* New York, Appleton, 1968.

32. Lowell Martin. *Students and the Pratt Library: Challenge and Opportunity.* Baltimore, Md., Enoch Pratt Free Library, 1963. (pamphlet)

33. Jeanne Shall. *Learning to Read; the Great Debate.* New York, McGraw, 1967.

34. Esther Baur. "The Fader Plan: Detroit Style", *Library Journal,* Sept. 15, 1967, p. 3119.

35. "Concern on Smut Held Unfounded", *New York Times,* Aug. 6, 1970, p. 22.

36. L. C. Merritt. *Book Selection and Intellectual Freedom.* Wilson, 1970, p. 19.

FOR ADDITIONAL INFORMATION

LIBRARIES AND STUDENTS

"The Effective Secondary School Library." *Bulletin of the National Association of Secondary School Principals,* November, 1959. 230p.

"Libraries in Secondary Schools, A New Look." *Bulletin of the National Association of Secondary School Principals,* January 1966. 122p.

New Definitions of School Library Service, edited by Sara I. Fenwick. Chicago, American Library Association, 1960. 90p.

Standards for School Library Programs. Chicago, American Library Association, 1960. 132p.

Standards for School Media Programs. Chicago, American Library Association, 1969. 66p.

Student Use of Libraries: An Inquiry Into the Needs of Students, Libraries, and the Educational Process. Chicago, American Library Association, 1964. 212p.

LIBRARIES AND THE NEW MEDIA

Educational Media in Libraries, edited by Carl Melinat. Syracuse, N.Y., Syracuse University, School of Library Service, 1963. 39p.

Guides to Newer Educational Media, by Margaret I. Rufsvold and Carolyn Guss. 2d ed. Chicago, American Library Association, 1967. 62p. (3d ed. announced for summer 1971).

Instructional Materials Centers: Selected Readings, by N.P. Pearson and Lucius Butler. Minneapolis, Minn., Burgess Pub. Co., 1969. 345p.

"Library Uses of the New Media of Communication", edited by C. Walter Stone. *Library Trends,* October 1967. 120p.

The School Library as a Materials Center, edited by Mary Helen Mahar. (Office of Education Circular No. 708) Washington, D.C., U.S. Govt. Print. Off., 1963. 84p.

THE SCHOOL LIBRARY AND EDUCATIONAL CHANGE

The School Library Materials Center: Its Resources and Their Utilization, edited by Alice Lohrer. Champaign, Ill., Illini Union Bookstore, 1964. 109p.

The School Library: Facilities for Independent Study in the Secondary School, by R.E. Ellsworth and H.D. Wagener. Edited by Ruth Weinstock. New York, Educational Facilities Laboratory, 1963. 143p.

The Teacher and the Machine, by P.W. Jackson. Pittsburgh, Pittsburgh University Press, 1968. 90p.

Technology in Education. Hearings before the Subcommittee of the Joint Economic Committee, Congress of the United States. Washington, D.C., U.S. Govt. Print. Off., 1966. 273p.

BOOKS AND SCHOOL LIBRARIES

Books and the Teen Age Reader: A Guide for Teachers, Librarians, and Parents, by G.R. Carlsen. New York, Bantam, 1967. 218p. (under revision)

Books in the Schools, edited by James Cass. New York, American Book Publishers Council, 1961. 65p.

Books, Young People, and Reading Guidance, by G.R. Hanna and M.K. McAllister. 2d ed. New York, Harper, 1968. 241p.

Hooked on Books: Program and Proof, by Daniel N. Fader and Elton B. McNeill. New York, Berkley, 1968. 236p.

Individualized Reading Instruction: Its Implications for the Teacher and Librarian, by Roland West. Port Washington, N.Y., Kennikat Press, 1964. 168p.

Individualizing Your Reading Program, by Jeanette Veatch. New York, Putnam, 1959. 242p.

Paperbacks in Education, edited by Vivienne Anderson. New York, Teachers College Press, 1966. 203p.

FOR ADDITIONAL INFORMATION

LIBRARY INSTRUCTION

Instructional Materials for Teaching the Use of the Library. A Selected Annotated Bibliography of Films, Filmstrips, Books and Pamphlets, Tests and Other Aids. 2d ed., by Shirley L. Hopkinson. San Jose, Calif., Claremont House, 1967. 59p.

The Library in High School Teaching, by Martin Rossoff. 2d ed. New York, Wilson, 1961. 166p.

INDEX

INDEX